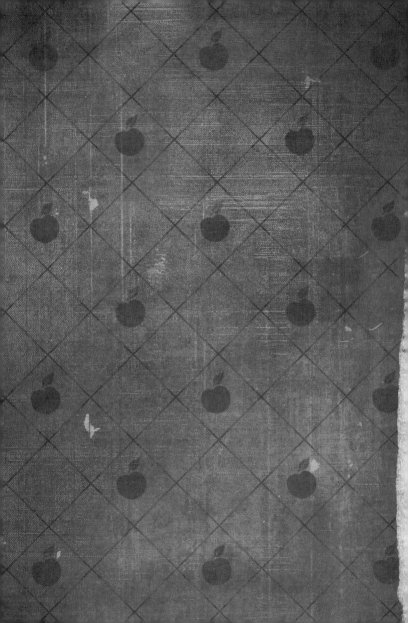

AN APPLE A DAY

365 Devotions for the Heart of a Teacher

Kathy Branzell

BroadStreet
PUBLISHING

BroadStreet Publishing Group, LLC
Savage, MN, USA
BroadStreetPublishing.com

An Apple a Day: 365 Devotions for the Heart of a Teacher (2nd Edition)

Cover design by Chris Garborg at garborgdesign.com
Typesetting by Katherine Lloyd at theDESKonline.com
Assistant Editors: Sandy Albrycht, Amy McDonald, and Nathanael White

Printed in China

19 20 21 22 22 5 4 3 2 1

To the thousands of educators who change the world one student at a time. I am so thankful for you and especially for all the teachers who poured into my life and my children. I want to give special thanks to the members of FACE for Educators, CEAI, and Compass, all laboring with love in the fields of education and to all the Moms in Prayer who are praying for schools around the world. Blessings!

Introduction

Dear Educator,

I have been blessed with so many wonderful teachers and coaches in my lifetime. From my preschool years through post-graduate education, my mind and character have been covered in the fingerprints of amazing educators who touched their students with love as well as learning. The inspiration provided was often as important as the information given to me and the countless others who walked into their classroom.

It was such a sweet gift to write these devotionals to you. As a teacher for over a decade, and with seventeen more years in education ministry, I have had the privilege to pray with thousands of educators and to hear their stories and prayer requests through the years. I pray that *An Apple a Day* helps you feel encouraged and appreciated, as well as conveys some new ideas and wisdom on how to live out your faith on the mission field of education. I am praying for you!

Serving Him with gladness,
Kathy Branzell

August

All

I can do all things through Him who strengthens me.
—PHILIPPIANS 4:13

Most of us have quoted this verse at some point in our life. Some of us may even recite this verse when going to work or going home every day. Sometimes we feel like our "all things" are too much. Other times we feel like our "all things" is too big.

As educators, it feels as if we get two starts to a new year. We get a new year on January first like everyone else, but we also get a new year on the first day of school. We get a chance to start fresh, make new plans, and set new goals. What "all things" would you like to do this year that will take His strength?

There's a huge difference between activity and accomplishment. Our days get filled, and if we don't control our schedule, it will control us. Our days fly by. Before long, May will be here and we'll find ourselves saying, "Where did this year go?" Pray and complete this sentence: "I can _____ through Him who strengthens me."

> Jesus, I know that I can do all that you call me to do, through your strength. Amen.

Dedicated and Devoted

Protect me, for I am devoted to you. Save me, for I serve you and trust you. You are my God. —Psalm 86:2 NLT

Thank you for being here today. God is delighted to see you take time to read His Word and pray. He is eager to hear your prayers and to speak His purpose, guidance, and comfort to you as His presence permeates this place. He would not miss this meeting for anything!

Whether this is your first year or fiftieth year teaching, I want to challenge you to dedicate yourself and this year to the Lord. This is perhaps the most important commitment you will make all year. Pray in and around your school, through your classroom and your rosters, saying a prayer of dedication committing the entire year to Jesus.

I want to encourage you to take what you learn in your prayer and devotional time, and apply it in life and your classroom. Know and exercise your legal rights but stay within the law; you have more religious room than you might think.

> Lord, I dedicate this year to your plans and glory.
> I am your servant. Amen.

God Supplies

And my God will supply every need of yours according to
His riches in glory in Christ Jesus. –PHILIPPIANS 4:19

I love new school supplies! I hope I never lose the excitement of opening a brand-new box of crayons or feeling the cut of a new pair of scissors. I pray that all your students have the resources to start the year with new supplies, but if you have needs, contact local churches; they often collect and distribute school supplies for students who cannot afford them.

Educators also need new "supplies" as we greet another year of students' personalities and learning styles. You may need some new teaching tools and definitely fresh prayers in addition to using all our experiences and education from years past.

Please know that I am praying that God will supply you with all that you need. I hear from teachers all over the world who go through the entire year and never feel fully equipped to do their jobs. God knows what you need long before classroom rosters are typed up; He will supply all your needs, fully and faithfully. Just ask Him.

Lord, may I always see—and share—
how you supply all my needs. Amen.

New

The LORD's lovingkindnesses indeed never cease,
for His compassions never fail. They are new every
morning; great is Your faithfulness. –LAMENTATIONS 3:22–23

This may be your first year as an educator, or you may be at a new school; if so, all things are *new*! Or perhaps this is a time of great change in your school or district–new administration, curriculums, expectations, and so on.

The word *next* invokes ideas of forward movement. *Next* comes with anticipation of another breath, step, day, or accomplishment in the journey or the race toward a goal (or at least the finish line). So what's new with you? What are you experiencing for the first time or with fresh eyes and a fresh attitude? What is your next step toward your goal?

The new school year is a clean slate, a chance to be the teacher you always wanted to be, to accomplish that personal goal you have always dreamed about, or to tackle that "thing" that stands between you and whatever you're striving for (peace, success, financial security, dream come true, and so on). With God by your side, go for it!

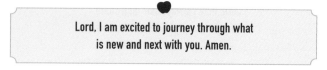

Lord, I am excited to journey through what
is new and next with you. Amen.

School Supplies

Now he who supplies seed to the sower and bread for food
will also supply and multiply your seed for storing and
increase the harvest of your righteousness.
—2 CORINTHIANS 9:10 ESV

For fun today, here are some verses for you to ponder as you process all the new supplies being brought into your classroom:

- *Ruler.* Luke 6:38: "Give, and it will be given to you.
  A good *measure* pressed down, shaken together and
  running over, will be poured into your lap. For with the
  measure you use, it will be measured to you" (NIV).
- *Glue and pencils.* Deuteronomy 11:18: "*Fix* these words of
  mine in your hearts and minds; tie them as symbols on
  your hands and *bind* them on your foreheads" (NIV).
- *Scissors.* Psalm 129:4: "But the LORD is righteous; he has
  cut me free from the cords of the wicked" (NIV).
- *Crayons.* Isaiah 1:18: "Though your sins are like *scarlet,*
  they shall be as *white* as snow; though they are *red* as
  crimson, they shall be like wool" (NIV). Psalm 23:2:
  "He makes me lie down in *green* pastures" (NIV).

Lord, please bless and multiply my supplies
to expand learning and righteousness. Amen.

Welcome

Whoever welcomes one of these little children in my name welcomes me; and whoever welcomes me does not welcome me but the one who sent me. –MARK 9:37 NIV

I pray you had a wonderful and restful summer. As you are welcoming a new year and students, welcome Jesus into your school and classroom. Take a prayer walk around and through your school, praying for this year, the students, the staff and administration, the school board and district workers, buses, curriculum, parents, finances, and anything else you can think of. Welcome God into your school, and invite Him to join you every day in the classrooms and hallways.

Then, welcome new teachers, staff, or administrators to your school. It can be difficult being the new anything on campus. Transition can be painful or pleasant depending on the relationships and circumstances. Give your new team members a chance, and keep your mind and door open to them. Pray for them and your school, because change is difficult for all of you.

Last but certainly not least, welcome your students' parents. Children's success rates increase when their parents are involved at school.

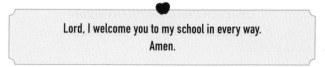

Lord, I welcome you to my school in every way.
Amen.

A Letter to the Church on School Campuses

The LORD bless you and keep you; the LORD make his face to shine upon you and be gracious to you; the LORD lift up his countenance upon you and give you peace. –NUMBERS 6:24–26 ESV

During his ministry, the apostle Paul wrote letters to several different communities, and his love for Jesus and his relationship with each church permeated his words. Using a portion of 1 Corinthians 1, personalize a letter as if you were writing it to your school campus, and add your comments and blessings since you know the needs of your campus:

> [Your name], called to be a servant of Christ Jesus by the will of God, to the church of God on school campuses around the world, to those who have been sanctified in Christ Jesus, saints by calling, with all who in every place call on the name of our Lord Jesus Christ, their Lord and ours: Grace to you and peace from God our Father and the Lord Jesus Christ. I thank my God always concerning you for the grace of God which was given you in Christ Jesus, that in everything you were enriched in Him, in all speech and all knowledge.

Lord, continue to grow your church
on school campuses. Amen.

Again I Say ...

> "Again I say to you, if two of you agree on earth about anything they ask, it will be done for them by my Father in heaven." —MATTHEW 18:19 ESV

In this verse, Jesus, the Teacher whose example we seek to follow every day, reminds us again of the power of prayer. He essentially begins with, "Again, I tell you …" Oh, the number of times a teacher has said that!

Even Jesus has students who need lessons repeated. Maybe you're one of them. Sometimes we learn just by reading and remembering, but many times we learn by doing—through repetitive reminders or even the occasional "hard way."

Perhaps you tend to be "gifted" when it comes to the Lord's lessons. Do you often need some one-on-one tutoring, or do you fall somewhere in the "proficient" range? (Just a little "testing" lingo to get you thinking ahead for the prayers you will need during those weeks of state testing.) Either way, make a point to find at least one other person at your school to pray with on a regular basis.

> Lord, please help me to find a friend
> to pray with at school. Amen.

Ambassadors

For God was in Christ, reconciling the world to himself,
no longer counting people's sins against them. And he
gave us this wonderful message of reconciliation. So we are
Christ's ambassadors; God is making his appeal through us.
—2 CORINTHIANS 5:19–20 NLT

An ambassador is a representative, an official messenger with a special mission. As a Christian, you have the greatest mission of all: to share the love and message of Jesus everywhere you go. You are His ambassador at home, at school, when shopping, when working out, and when hanging out with friends. As a citizen of heaven, you are His ambassador on earth; your words and actions represent Him and what it means to be a part of His family and kingdom.

Exhibit His love, share His peace, and show people how wonderful it is to be forgiven and reconciled instead of exiled. Speak His words and live His ways with joy and strength. Be mindful of your position as His ambassador, and know that He is delighted to have you sharing His wonderful message on this special mission.

> Lord, thank you for making me an ambassador
> of your kingdom. May I represent you well. Amen.

Great Grace

> But God, who is rich in mercy, because of His great love
> that He had for us, made us alive with the Messiah even
> though we were dead in trespasses. By grace you are saved!
> —Ephesians 2:4–5 hcsb

It is by God's grace through Christ's atoning sacrifice that we are saved. It is not our accomplishments and successes, or lack of these, that decide our eternal fate—thank God! Grace, by definition, is undeserved. We cannot earn salvation or grace; it is granted to us.

What a wonderful gift it would be if you let your students enter your school and classroom washed "new" in grace this year, with a clean slate! Imagine pulling them out from under the thundercloud of past mistakes, bad choices, and a less-than-stellar reputation, and allowing them to walk warmly welcomed into your classroom with a bright future. Don't let their past cloud your view of the potential that shines in all of God's children.

> Lord, thank you for your grace that lifted me out of
> the pit of sin and into your plan and presence. Prompt me
> to encourage my students with great grace. Amen.

Good Gifts

> "If you then, being evil, know how to give good gifts to
> your children, how much more will your Father who is in
> heaven give what is good to those who ask Him!"
> —MATTHEW 7:11

Know your heavenly Father. Know He loves you and only acts through His love for you. Know that He knows what is best and that you will be blessed by whatever He is blessing you to receive. You must come to Him with a humble, "Please," not an entitled, "Give me."

When you pray for blessings, opportunities, increase, and such, do you find yourself thinking or even telling God exactly what that blessing should look like? When Jesus said to His disciples, "Come follow Me," they immediately followed Him. They didn't ask for a three-year plan for the journey. So why do we find it so hard to obey and follow Him on this side of the cross? Trust His plans, and trust His hands to grip you and equip you.

Where do your greatest gifts and blessings come from? They come from God, of course.

Lord, I know that you only give good gifts.
Amen.

Grow and Glorify

But grow in the grace and knowledge of our Lord and
Savior Jesus Christ. To him be glory both now and forever!
Amen. −2 PETER 3:18 NIV

Sometimes growth is fun and exciting, and your heart swells with gratefulness and love. Sometimes growth is difficult and painful, but He is faithful, and your heart enlarges yet again, with maturing faith, gratefulness, and love. Growth occurs when we learn something new, understand something deeper, and apply wisdom where there was once confusion. Growth occurs when we walk on the waves of life, through the storm of sickness, on the sea of sorrow, or in shadow of disappointment or death. Growth occurs when we overcome addiction, loss, or earthly abandonment, and thankfully, it also comes in the joy-filled days, the new beginnings, the second chances, and the once-in-a-life-time opportunities.

How would you like to grow this year? Write down a personal "snapshot" of yourself—a picture of words that describes where you are—and addresses some of the questions and opportunities for growth.

Lord, I want to grow and glorify you every day.
Amen.

Effective

I thank my God always, making mention of you
in my prayers, because I hear of your love and of the faith
which you have toward the Lord Jesus and toward the
saints; and I pray that the fellowship of your faith may
become effective through the knowledge of every good
thing which is in you for Christ's sake. –PHILEMON 4–6

Do you have an individual or group of people who pray *for* you? Every day for over eighteen years I have prayed for teachers and other school staff daily. Knowing there is always someone on their knees interceding for you through everything you face is a powerful experience.

Do you have someone on your campus to pray *with* you? Prayer groups meet in their own schools all across America to share things they cannot share elsewhere–things about family, dreams, struggles, fears, and victories–knowing that what is shared will only be spoken of before God.

It is this prayerful community that I believe leads us–Christian educators–to become so effective in our schools that those around us wonder at what God does through us. Ask someone to pray for you and with you today.

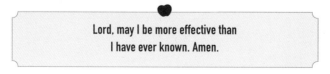

Lord, may I be more effective than
I have ever known. Amen.

How Should I Pray Today?

If we don't know how or what to pray, it doesn't matter.
He does our praying in and for us, making prayer out of
our wordless sighs, our aching groans. –ROMANS 8:26 MSG

Sometimes we don't know what to say when we pray. Sometimes we pray with sobs and other times with Scripture; no matter what, the important thing is to always pray.

Pray God's will be done on earth as it is in heaven. Pray God's authority over all people and circumstances—that He would be recognized as Sovereign God, Creator, and Redeemer. Pray that all people would seek to obey and glorify Him, and that our nation would bless Him. Pray that He would strengthen us, His followers, to speak truth in love; to love Him with all our heart, soul, mind, and strength; and to love our neighbor as ourselves. Pray that His love would shine light in dark places, and that all things done in the darkness of corruption, destruction, and pride would be exposed. Pray that all would repent and follow Jesus, and that comfort would come now and in eternal life.

> Lord, let your Spirit speak my heart when
> I don't know what to say. Amen.

Complete Rest

The LORD spoke to Moses, saying, "But as for you,
speak to the sons of Israel, saying, 'You shall surely observe
My sabbaths; for this is a sign between Me and you
throughout your generations, that you may know that
I am the LORD who sanctifies you.'" –EXODUS 31:12–13

God created us. Knowing full well what we would need, He was adamant that we rest, so He commanded (not suggested) that His people rest one full day per week. We need to rest if we are going to reach our full potential and serve Him as living love letters to the least and the lost.

I must confess that all too often I get distressed, wondering where time went and why I didn't accomplish everything I had on my to-do list. I realized it was because I either had too many things on my to-do list or I was not obeying God's call to rest and trust that He would bless my obedience throughout the other six days. I needed to heed God's command to rest more and let Him lighten my load.

I challenge you to observe the Sabbath and see how God blesses your rest.

Lord, thank you for teaching us
to experience complete rest. Amen.

Humble

Therefore humble yourselves under the mighty hand
of God, that He may exalt you at the proper time, casting
all your anxieties on Him, because He cares about you.
–1 Peter 5:6–7

My daughter, Emily, had been so excited that we were having country fried steak, but now she sat with her head in her hands, elbows on the table, and her eyebrows drawn in a scowl. Why the change in attitude? Because at age five, she was determined to cut up her own steak by herself. As excitement quickly changed to anger and frustration, I suggested she ask her father to help her since he would be happy to do so. She groaned and continued to pout. Her desire to do it herself kept her from enjoying her favorite dinner.

How many times do we miss an opportunity, or miss blessings, because we refuse to ask our heavenly Father for His help? You've probably had students who needed help but refused to ask. Likewise, at the beginning of the school year or a new task, we start out enthusiastic and then soon find ourselves with our head in our hands and a scowl on our face. Meanwhile, God sits as close to us as Emily's dad was to her, waiting to help if we would just ask.

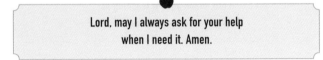

Lord, may I always ask for your help
when I need it. Amen.

Just Sayin'

"You have heard that it was said, 'You shall love
your neighbor and hate your enemy.' But I say to you,
love your enemies and pray for those who persecute you."
—MATTHEW 5:43–44

Jesus made several "You have heard it said ... but I say to you ..." statements. He trumps tradition, culture, and current trends. He is sovereign, and listening to what He says will keep us safe and successful in all the plans He has for us. Satan, on the other hand, has a plan for us too; he wants to do everything he can to trip and tie us up so we're distracted and detained.

Jesus says things like, "All things are possible with Me," "Trust Me," "Persevere," and "Press on." He encourages, while satan discourages. Jesus gives us the strength that satan wants to drain from us. He sets dreams in our heart, while evil sets doubt in our mind. Jesus promises to protect us, while the enemy will try to fill us with fear. Bad counsel will try to justify sin and may lead us to "bend the rules" just a bit. But Jesus says, "If you love Me, you will obey Me."

Lord, may I always obey what I hear you say.
Amen.

Filled by His Presence

You make known to me the path of life; in your presence
there is fullness of joy; at your right hand are pleasures
forevermore. –PSALM 16:11 ESV

Practicing His presence means saturating our life with His Word.
It is a practice of studying His Word every day, a practice that,
like a physical workout, grows longer and stronger as we seek to
grow in His presence. It is a healthy fear of the Lord–not a run-
away-scared fear, but an awe-filled respect of His authority that
is our guard and guide when we are practicing His presence, and
our discipline when we are escaping.

Practicing God's presence means spending time focused on
Him. It means that we are dedicated to time in prayer and studying His Word. We cannot go to church for an hour or two each
week, hoping to put something in our tank that we can run on
all week. We always come hoping for a good filling or at least
good feelings, but the feelings fade and the filling turns to fumes
because we need Him to fill us every minute of every day.

Lord, fill me with your presence.
Amen.

Hesed

Then he said, "May you be blessed of the LORD,
my daughter. You have shown your last kindness
to be better than the first." –RUTH 3:10

The book of Ruth is amazing. It's a story of tragedy and triumph that begins with three women widowed. The newly widowed daughter-in-law Ruth vows to remain and live out her days with her mother-in-law, Naomi.

If you study the text, you will find the Hebrew word *hesed,* translated as kindness repeated throughout the story. *Hesed* is defined as loyal love, goodness, covenant faithfulness, mercy, grace, benevolence, and kindness. Notice also that the definition says *and,* not *or.* *Hesed* is all of these traits rolled up into one—one big word, one big emotion, and one big action all in one. It is part of your character and commitment.

God responds to our prayers and needs because of His *hesed.* He also looks to His people to practice *hesed* in their relationships, and He rewards them for it. But *hesed* also carries its own reward: it is contagious. When you receive it, it makes you want to give it.

Who do you know who needs *hesed* today?

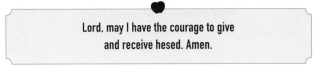

Lord, may I have the courage to give
and receive hesed. Amen.

Changing the Culture

"Your kingdom come, your will be done, on earth
as it is in heaven." –MATTHEW 6:10 ESV

The verse above is the believer's deepest desire—for God to be awed, obeyed, and glorified in our lives, homes, schools, city, state, county, and culture, as He is in heaven. Oh, that we could see and understand God the way His angels do in heaven! We would never doubt, disobey, or deny Him access to a part of our lives ever again.

For now, the world looks to Jesus' followers in their attempt to understand Jesus. We must abide in unity under God's authority, and then speak and live by His authority, taking every opportunity to be a godly influence to every person and place as God guides and provides.

Take a good look at the culture of your school campus. What would it look like for His kingdom to come and His will to be done there as it is in heaven? Pray about it.

Lord, I will walk and work in humility, unity,
and your authority and influence on my campus,
in my community, and beyond. Amen.

Know, Grow, and Sow

The righteous man will flourish like the palm tree,
he will grow like a cedar in Lebanon. Planted in the house
of the LORD, they will flourish. –PSALM 92:12–13

If you've attended a Bible study, you probably noticed that everyone didn't come into the class with the same level of knowledge, understanding, and training. We're all at different places in our journey with Jesus. It's important for new believers to hear about experiences of seasoned believers and to learn from their knowledge and witness their faith. On the other hand, it's also important for seasoned believers to be rejuvenated by the curiosity and energy of new believers.

God does not expect us to learn and live at the same pace, just as your students learn at different paces and levels. It's important to know that He loves us all the same. We all have equal access to Him, and His gifts are poured out through His Spirit as He determines His purposes in each life. He has also blessed us with Christian brothers and sisters to educate and encourage us on our journey.

Lord, help me to gather with believers
to know, grow, and sow together. Amen.

What Do You Want?

Jesus stopped and called them. "What do you want me
to do for you?" he asked. —MATTHEW 20:32 NIV

Jesus asked two blind men, "What do you want me to do for
you?" We would think the answer should be obvious, and it
was: they asked for their sight.

Does Jesus know what you want with regard to your students?
Of course, but He also wants you to ask Him for it. To help you
appeal to Him for them you could begin with this prayer:

Thank you, Jesus, for these students. Let my contact
with them reverberate across their lives. May they know
that they're wonderfully made and priceless, and I pray
they will fully value the wonderful, priceless people they
meet. May they know they are loved and should love
others. Help them reach for their dreams but not miss
rewards on the way. Let me show them that helping others feels so much better than putting them down. Show
them value in the differences of people so they won't
believe that everyone should be like them. Make them
yearn to learn and seek you always, living life with an
open heart and wise choices.

Lord, may I always remember that you always want
to hear from me, no matter the day or time. Amen.

Chew on the Review

Then he left them, got back into the boat and crossed
to the other side. The disciples had forgotten to bring bread,
except for one loaf they had with them in the boat.
—MARK 8:13–14 NIV

Sailing on the water, He had previously commanded, "Be still!" and had continued on. Then Jesus listened again to His disciples worry about where their next meal would come from. It's no wonder He asked, "Are your hearts hardened? Do you have eyes but fail to see, and ears but fail to hear? And don't you remember?" (Mark 8:17–18 NIV). So Jesus took them through a quick review: How could they worry about food when they saw Jesus supply bread for over nine thousand people in two recent situations?

Sadly, in the same way, we worry about things that He has taken care of for us time and time again. We forget. All the disciples needed was there on the boat, and He is all we need as well. We frequently review material with students so they don't forget it. The cure for our worry is to review His faithfulness and celebrate instead of worrying about where our next bite of bread or blessing will come from.

Lord, may I regularly review all that
Jesus has done for me. Amen.

Grow Toward His Glory

For everyone has sinned; we all fall short
of God's glorious standard. –ROMANS 3:23 NLT

How do you react when you make a mistake? Do you learn a quick lesson, ask for forgiveness, and move on, or do you harp on it, call yourself names, and let it weigh you down for days, weeks, or years? For some reason, we tend to beat ourselves up when we make mistakes.

Sometimes people make an "honest" mistake—one that is completely unintentional. Other mistakes are made out of pride, greed, or retaliation. Both result in a lesson and the need for forgiveness.

You've probably heard Romans 3:23 recited many times. It provides the "I'm just human" excuse to our sin, but we cannot stop there. God does not forgive based on an excuse; He forgives based on Romans 3:24. We "are justified by his grace as a gift, through the redemption that is in Christ Jesus." God wants a heartfelt apology and repentance, but forgiveness is granted by grace. The price has already been paid, and we cannot add to it.

Jesus, forgive me for _____. I receive your
grace and grow toward your glory. Amen.

Experience and Express God's Unchanging Goodness

I will bless the LORD at all times; His praise shall
continually be in my mouth. … O taste and see that the
LORD is good; how blessed is the man who takes
refuge in Him! –PSALM 34:1, 8

This psalm is a pledge of faithfulness to a faithful God. The commitment rolls off the psalmist's heart and tongue: "I will bless the Lord."

Precious friends, I want to submit to you that this is the recipe for a happy life. The psalmist commits to do this continually. He reminds us that our unchanging God is truly good. Just take that in for a moment. Here is a promise that all who take refuge in God will receive His goodness, but what does it mean to take refuge in God?

Taking refuge in God is an everyday decision to stay under His wings of authority and shelter with confidence that our hope is in Him, not some wish or positive thinking ruled by happenstance and coincidences. Think about what this would look like in your life.

Lord, I take refuge in you and reflect on your faithfulness.
May I always reveal the fruit of your faithfulness to others
so that they too may taste and see that you are good. Amen.

The Staying Power of Love

The chief priests also, along with the scribes, were mocking Him among themselves and saying, "He saved others; He cannot save Himself." –MARK 15:31

Jesus could have saved Himself, but instead He chose to save us. He not only defeated death for Himself but for all who believe! His love defied understanding and reached across centuries of sin-saturated people in desperate need of a Savior, but it was carried out in the midst of hatred and insults. This is the staying power of *love*.

As an educator, you have probably been mocked, insulted, and disrespected as you sacrificed to teach. Your students don't rush into class every day bearing gifts and speaking praise and thanks. Parents are not leaving piles of cash on your desk to repay you for pouring into their child's future. You are an educator because of *love*; you love God, and He called you to this mission field. Love remained on the cross, and love remains in the classroom. Thank you for having that kind of sacrificial love, because this is the love that changes the world.

Jesus, saturate me in the staying power
of your love for your glory. Amen.

Make Glad

Anxiety in a man's heart weighs him down,
but a good word makes him glad. –Proverbs 12:25 esv

Here is yet another example in Scripture of the power of our words. How awesome it is to think that we have the ability to make someone glad. What would you pay to see someone smile—your friend, spouse, students, or even strangers who are hurting? The beautiful thing is that you can make it happen for free; kind words don't cost anything but a few moments of time. God created us with the ability to love and lift one another up.

You may be the only person to speak encouragement into someone's life. It may not be the first thing that comes to mind when that student is sitting outside the principal's office—*again*—or has failed another test, but your good words could become the moment in their life when they determine to turn their lives around or work harder. Your words can turn around a day or even a life.

Lord, let all that I say make glad hearts
and better lives. Amen.

Acknowledge

> Trust in the LORD with all your heart and do not
> lean on your own understanding. In all your ways
> acknowledge Him, and He will make your paths straight.
> —PROVERBS 3:5–6

The Hebrew word for *acknowledge* is *yada*, pronounced "yaw-dah." It means know, learn to know, perceive, distinguish, know by experience, recognize, confess, consider, cause to know, and declare.

Now read the verse ten more times, each time using a different definition from above in place of the word *acknowledge*: "In all your ways _____ Him, and He will make your paths straight."

In your classroom, you want your students to do all these things with the subject you're teaching. The more of these they master, the better they know, understand, and can apply the material.

We all have something we need to acknowledge about God today—His power, His love, His plan for our life, His forgiveness, His presence. What others can you name? Acknowledge your love for Him now.

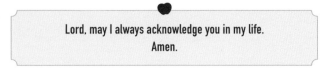

Lord, may I always acknowledge you in my life.
Amen.

Plow Season

Sluggards do not plow in season; so at harvest time
they look but find nothing. —PROVERBS 20:4 NIV

There are some seasons of life that seem more hectic than others. The beginning of the school year can be chaotic as we try to set a routine and pace for our classroom. This is a "plowing season," where we work hard so the ground is prepared to plant seeds of progress.

Think about what you do during this season to prepare your students for success. Expectations must be spoken and sustained for order and budding academic achievement to take root. Healthy roots bring good fruit. Teach students from plowing to harvest. We reap what we sow, so exemplify how every day matters. Breaking huge tasks into day-by-day steps nurtures everyone.

Prayer is the greatest nutrient, kind of like Miracle-Gro. Any good farmer will tell you he prays because there is so much he cannot control. He can toil, but in the end, only God brings a harvest. He has called you to plow and nurture. Pray on!

Jesus, help me to prepare, plow, and nurture
for your abundant harvest. Amen.

Little Miracles

> Jesus said, "Let the little children come to me,
> and do not hinder them, for the kingdom of heaven
> belongs to such as these." —MATTHEW 19:14 NIV

Our students are little (and sometimes not-so-little) miracles with backpacks. All of them are special, full of wonder with an amazing future ahead, if we just persevere and equip them. Some need more love and patience than others. Some need more time and creative intervention to learn. None are hopeless; God does not create "lost causes."

As adults, sometimes we forget the magic of our childhood years; we give up hope too soon and tend to forget why we became educators. We need to keep our heart and focus on the miracle of each life and soul that God has placed in our path. We must trek through the tough times and tough exteriors to complete the task God has entrusted to us.

Dig deep into your heart to find the inspiration and motivation of your first day of teaching, then prepare your students for the rest of their lives and eternity.

> Lord, open my eyes and heart to continue to see "little miracles"—hearts and souls formed by your hands. Amen.

Reason

> "Come now, and let us reason together," says the LORD,
> "Though your sins are as scarlet, they will be as white
> as snow; … If you consent and obey, you will eat the best of
> the land; but if you refuse and rebel, you will be devoured."
> —ISAIAH 1:18–20

Have you ever asked your students to give you a *reason* for something they did or said? And what do you expect if you ask someone to be *reasonable*?

God calls us to His compassion and forgiveness, but the free will He gives us provides the choice to obey or rebel. The word *reason* in Hebrew is *yakach*, and it means to prove, correct, be right, decide, reprove, and judge. God summons us to judge what is right—to choose wisely—because once we make a choice, it becomes a decision that we must walk and work out.

So, come. Spend the next moments and days reasoning with God. Ask Him for wisdom, knowledge, and understanding. Ask Him to give you clarity where things have been blurry, and to shine His light on the path He designed and desires for you.

> Lord, please help me to make right choices
> and divine decisions. Amen.

September

A Good Neighbor

Let each of us please his neighbor for his good,
to build him up. —ROMANS 15:2 ESV

We are flooded with pictures of and information about celebrities in triumph and turmoil—on magazine covers, in entertainment "news," and on talk shows. Their affairs, relationships, divorces, pregnancies, break-ups, makeups, slip-ps, and any other tidbit of pain or gossip are displayed for all to see. But they need prayer, not publicity.

Think about what would happen if we knew more about what was occurring in the lives of our neighbors than we did about the lives of celebrities. Or if we prayed more about our relationships and the potential relationships around us as well as for the famous.

How much do you know about the new teachers or staff hired at your school this year? Consider what this year might look like if you concentrated on building these people up, and if you focused your good words and deeds on the people you pass by every day.

Lord, I pray that entertainers will use their talent and influence for your glory. Help me find opportunities to build up the people in my neighborhood, school, and church. Amen.

Abide Not Hide

He who dwells in the shelter of the Most High
will abide in the shadow of the Almighty. I will say
to the LORD, "My refuge and my fortress, My God,
in whom I trust!" –PSALM 91:1–2

What makes your heart pound and your palms sweat? For lack of a better word, what do you fear?

I fear doing new things and going new places, but there is also an underlying fear that causes those fears. I fear letting God down, and I fear failure. You'd never know this since I travel almost every week of the year. So what have I learned that keeps me serving on the move?

I've found that when fear tries to grab me, something wonderful is about to happen. The only real failure is not trying at all. God's children abide in His shadow; we are not weak-willed wimps who run and hide. Facing our fears is an act of faith. Change only comes by faith–trusting God and moving forward. If we are frozen with fear, satan scores. Fight fear with faith.

> Lord, may I courageously abide in
> the shelter of your shadow. Amen.

An Intellectual Introduction

"For while I was passing through and examining the objects
of your worship, I also found an altar with this inscription,
'TO AN UNKNOWN GOD.' Therefore what you worship
in ignorance, this I proclaim to you." –ACTS 17:23

Paul spoke these words to begin his sermon on Mars Hill in
Athens, where he used the culture as a tool to testify to the one
true God, Creator of heaven and earth.

As educators, we can learn from Paul's example of using what
is visible and familiar to our students to teach them about the invisible and unfamiliar. You can use this method to introduce some
of your students to a God that is "unknown" to them.

You might be surprised to know that your state standards, the
Supreme Court, the PTA, and the NEA all expect, and in some
cases even require, that you teach about Christian concepts, stories, traditions, history, and contributions, all in order to teach the
whole child with a whole education. If any of these revelations
interest you, you can learn more through Gateways to Better Education at www.gtbe.org.

Lord, thank you for the wisdom to dispel ignorance
through an intellectual introduction. Amen.

Glorifying or Garbage

You know when I sit and when I rise; you perceive
my thoughts from afar. —PSALM 139:2 NIV

Self-talk is the conversations we have with ourselves. It might
be a question like, "What was I thinking?" or it might be a
long conversation that lasts for hours, even days. Sometimes the
talk is reassuring: "God's got you, and you can do this!" But
unfortunately, a lot of what we say to ourselves, we would never
let someone say to a friend or someone we love. So why are we
so hard on ourselves? And where do we get these negative ideas?

God knows our thoughts. We must determine which thoughts
are garbage and which ones glorify Him. Self-talk is very powerful, and we need to be on guard over what we allow to pass
through—or get caught—in our heads.

What do you think about most? Are they positive or negative
thoughts? How do you redirect your thoughts to get your mind
on to something else? Keep in mind that if the words you're saying to yourself aren't words that our loving God would say to
you, it's time to silence them. Ask God to put His thoughts about
you in your mind instead.

> Lord, teach me your thoughts. Help me to replace the
> garbage I think with thoughts that glorify you. Amen.

Replace Garbage with Grace

How precious to me are your thoughts, God!
How vast is the sum of them! —PSALM 139:17 NIV

After we toss out the garbage thoughts, we must replace them with grace and truth. Memorize Scripture, pray, and find a friend and vow to say something affirming about one another every day. Seek out worship songs that remind you of who we are in Him, and don't forget that the most important truth is God's Word. God has a lot to say about His thoughts and actions toward us in His Word. Read it, memorize it, and meditate on it whenever a lie tries to bounce around in your head.

You are a treasure, you are beautiful, you are God's workmanship, and you were born with a vital, unique purpose. You were created in His image, precious and loved, and are worth His Son's life. He never wants to be separated from you, He will never leave you, and you are never beyond His help or forgiveness. He will equip you to do all that He has planned for you. Your worth is beyond compare, and your value is priceless! Never forget that.

Lord, may I meditate on your thoughts
and walk in your ways. Amen.

Confessing

He who conceals his transgressions will not prosper, but he who confesses and forsakes them will find compassion.
–PROVERBS 28:13

Showers with glass walls must be squeegeed after each shower to keep the glass clean and clear. Ignore it, and you deal with a thick scum that is difficult to see through and much more difficult to clean off.

The same is true for our hearts. Daily sin builds up on its walls and blocks our vision of God and His plan and purpose for our lives. Daily confession squeegees off the sinful residue and prevents destructive build-up that is much more difficult to deal with over time.

How can you help your students to see that living a life of good character is important? Do you ever overlook small changes in attitude or misbehaviors because you're too busy or don't want to deal with it—only to have to face much bigger problems in the days ahead? Are the consequences lighter if students confess instead of trying to cover up their involvement? Ask them what it means to have a clean conscience, and guide the discussion.

Lord, may I have a clean heart
through daily confession. Amen.

Grace and Mercy

Therefore let us draw near with confidence to the throne
of grace, so that we may receive mercy and find grace
to help in time of need. —HEBREWS 4:16

If you don't know the story of the prodigal son, you can read it
in Luke 15:11–32.

I once heard a pastor ask, "What if the younger son had met
up with his older brother first?" Think about that. What kind of
"welcome home" would he have received? Would the younger
son have even continued toward the house to see his father, or
would he have turned back never to be seen again? Wow, what
a thought!

Could you use some grace and mercy? Perhaps you know
someone who needs a little grace and mercy. How quick are you
to forgive someone who has hurt you? Has someone treated you
badly and *not* asked for your forgiveness? Would you be willing
to make the first move by treating them with kindness? Maybe
someone you know has strayed in some way and needs some
grace and mercy to help restore their walk with God. Or maybe
you could use some grace and mercy. I think we all could.

Lord, may I give and receive
grace and mercy. Amen.

Commissioned

Therefore, if anyone is in Christ, he is a new creation. ...
This is from God, who reconciled us to himself through
Christ and gave us the ministry of reconciliation: ...
God was reconciling the world to himself in Christ ...
We are therefore Christ's ambassadors.
—2 CORINTHIANS 5:17–20 NIV

Christ became sin that we might become God's righteousness!
Does that leave you speechless? Ponder it for a moment. He
also gave us the message of salvation. We have been chosen and
strategically placed in people's lives as Christ's ambassadors. Our
attitudes and actions could transform an entire generation.

Pray through your class rosters regularly, calling the students
by name. Here is a prompt to begin praying:

Father, (student's name) was created by you. Jesus died
for (student's name) that he/she could be reconciled to
you. You have commissioned me as Christ's ambassador into (student's name)'s life. Help me to see the way
you do, and show me how to love, teach, and guide
what you have authored. Amen.

Journal and give thanks throughout the year as you see God
answer your prayers.

> Lord, thank you that I am a new creation
> and commissioned in Christ. Amen.

Blessed with Boundaries

Blessed are those whose way is blameless, who walk
in the law of the LORD! Blessed are those who keep his
testimonies, who seek him with their whole heart, who also
do no wrong, but walk in his ways! –PSALM 119:1-3 ESV

Rules and boundaries are meant to protect us. Think about the
rules in your school and what purposes they serve. Why do
we tell students not to run in the halls? Why do we take measures
to limit what they can view on the Internet? Because we're trying
to protect them and keep them safe, just as God gave us His commands to protect us.

We know that children feel safer knowing their boundaries,
even if they try to push the limits once in a while. Lack of boundaries causes anxiety in people of all ages. Have you ever been giv-
en a responsibility but no instructions for doing it? How would
you know if you were succeeding or failing?

Be thankful that God's commands are clear. We are blessed
when we walk in the safety and blessings of His boundaries.

Lord, thank you that your path is clear.
May I always walk in your ways. Amen.

United in Prayer

They all met together and were constantly
united in prayer. —ACTS 1:14 NLT

On the fourth Wednesday in September, students hold See You at the Pole (SYATP), an event committed to global unity in Christ as students unite in intercession before God. We are legally protected in professing our faith, and it strengthens our joy to pray and fellowship with other Christians. It can also be terrifying for students, as non-Christian students taunt and harass them as they pray and live out their faith. We persevere knowing that satan's worst fear is the prayers of the faithful!

God's heart is delighted that you make time to meet with Him and unite in prayer. I urge you to guard your unity with other Christians; it was Christ's prayer that His followers be united in Him.

Help students to unite by posting information in your classroom and pointing them to SYATP.org. Then stand near and provide protection as they pray around the pole. Allow students to discuss SYATP experiences and encourage them to express their faith with love. It is important for you to know legal rights and boundaries, as it is our heart to stir up prayer, not controversy.

Jesus, help me and others at my school
to unite in prayer. Amen.

Remember the Sacrifice

Greater love has no one than this, that one lay down
his life for his friends. –JOHN 15:13

This is the anniversary of the terrorist attacks on the United
States on September 11, 2001. This week will be filled with
memories and pictures of that terrible day when we sat paralyzed
in front of our television screens or maybe even stood watching
with our own eyes as the day's events played out. Many of our
memories are filled with firefighters and police officers rushing
into burning buildings without a single selfish thought, determined to get to those who were in danger. They did not stop to
think about what might happen to them.

We could learn a lot from these heroes. Our world is filled
with people who are in danger of perishing for eternity. What
risks will you take to rush to an unsaved soul crying out for help?
The fires of hell are burning. What stops us from going?

Pray today for the families affected by the 9/11 attacks and
thank God for those who gave their lives in an effort to rescue
others on that day.

Lord, send your comfort and strength
as we remember. Amen.

The Way We Should Go

And pray to the LORD your God for us … that the LORD
your God may show us the way we should go, and the
thing that we should do. –JEREMIAH 42:2–3 ESV

Our middle school code of conduct prohibited inappropriate
language, but the hallways were saturated with cussing students. The assistant principal just shrugged her shoulders and
said, "It's the language of our culture." I couldn't believe my ears!
The language of whose culture?

As a society, we have become numb to some things that
should still shock us. Think about it. Do you allow students to
get away with behavior that you should discipline because, compared to other students' actions, it's "not that bad"? The problem
here is that if you don't respond to unsuitable behavior, how will
students know that no means no and not that no means you'll
look the other way? If you've been teaching for a while, perhaps
you've found that providing consistent discipline early on leads
to less issues as the year progresses.

We must be the example first and then lovingly teach and
hold tight to the rules and laws, extending forgiveness but with
discipline. Don't look the other way; show them the way.

Lord, help me to know and show
the way we should go. Amen.

Sow His Seed

"Listen! A farmer went out to sow his seed. … Still other seed fell on good soil. It came up, grew and produced a crop, multiplying thirty, sixty, or even a hundred times."
—MARK 4:3, 8 NIV

As an educator, you probably feel like you wear many hats—teacher, counselor, referee, and so on—but did you ever realize that you are also a farmer? We sow and nurture educational seeds, helping some lessons to take deeper root while others grow and strengthen in size. We are even blessed to see some bloom before our eyes, during those wonderful moments when students put lessons together and get it.

We also sow life seeds—discipline, manners, and skills that students need, like tying their shoes, respecting other people, and taking courage to try something new. Finally, we sow the seed of God's Word. Not all the seed will flourish, but take heart, for there is good soil in your classes to receive it.

Each year, look over your students and see them as your harvest field. Sow generously, and believe God's promise that there will be a harvest!

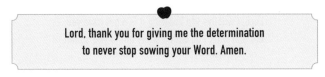

Lord, thank you for giving me the determination
to never stop sowing your Word. Amen.

Counting Our Days, Days that Count

So teach us to number our days, that we may present to You a heart of wisdom. –Psalm 90:12

We all want to get the most from our days. Even our students don't want their lives to be wasted, so we have to be deliberate. We desire something deeper than just showing up at school every day; we are focused on goals that act as a compass to where we want to go. Beyond setting goals, we must determine how to "spend" time. Every activity comes at the cost of another, and we often ask, "What's in it for me?"

Few opportunities allow us to receive without some sort of sacrifice or expense. Life comes in opportunities to give and take. If we plan to give, we can be more generous and cheerful in the process. Planning what and how we will give helps us to stay on the path to get the most out of life.

Ask your students what they hope to give and take this year, prompt a discussion about how they can fulfill these plans.

Lord, I will live life knowing it is a gift from you, and that what I do with it is my gift to you. Amen.

Be Glad

This is the day that the LORD has made;
let us rejoice and be glad in it. –PSALM 118:24 ESV

I am always surprised by the negative talk and discouraging discussions that pop up throughout the school year. Speak blessings and faith over your school and circumstances. Yes, the goals and expectations may be overwhelming. And you may be faced with a particular challenge either professionally or personally. But I encourage you to remember God's promises and His faithfulness. Wake up every morning and pray, "Lord, this is your day, and I am glad to be a part of it." Let that be the desire of your heart, and God will bless that prayer.

Every day has the possibility of taking your breath away. You get to decide if that is driven by fear or exhilarating faith, anxiety or anticipation. You get to choose if it will be an obstacle or an opportunity. God desires to draw you closer to Him so He can strengthen your faith, deepen your maturity, and journey with you through your destiny.

> Lord, may I rejoice and be glad in
> your hands each day. Amen.

Gladly Do Something New

"But forget all that—it is nothing compared to what
I am going to do. For I am about to do something new.
See, I have already begun! Do you not see it? I will
make a pathway through the wilderness."
—Isaiah 43:18–19 NLT

When was the last time you did something new? Educators everywhere are being asked to do several new things, not to ward off boredom but to help make them even better. Teachers and schools are in a constant pursuit for educational excellence.

God desires to do new things in you and through you. He will equip you for what you are required and responsible to do. Perhaps there are new things you're being asked to do in your job this year. Pray about them and get help from other educators; use your talents, and talk to teachers who have come from other schools that have already required some of these changes. Model the attitude of excitement for learning that you want students to have every day.

Lord, I want to gladly do something new.
Amen.

Yield

"Yield to the LORD and enter His sanctuary which
He has consecrated forever, and serve the LORD your God,
that His burning anger may turn away from you."
—2 CHRONICLES 30:8

When we're driving, *yield* means that we're supposed to slow down, and at times come to a complete stop, then wait until it's safe for us to proceed. It doesn't benefit anyone if we hurry and push our way out so everyone has to stop for us.

Scripture warns not to be stubborn and self-serving but to yield, or submit to God; pride has no place on His path. When we yield, wait, and watch, we can anticipate marvelous things that God can and will do. Sometimes our yielding is a short pause to check for permission; other times it's a long wait while God prepares our path before we proceed.

Think of a time in your life when yielding to think things through, pausing for prayer, and waiting for God probably would have kept you from a major life collision. Thank God for His work in your life while you wait on Him.

Lord, I yield to your will and ways. May I always
remember that your timing is perfect. Amen.

Visible Value

The eyes of the LORD are toward the righteous
and his ears toward their cry. –PSALM 34:15 ESV

You have more in common with your students than you might
think; for example, everyone wants to be noticed. It's not selfish to want people to recognize our existence and value. We want
people to take notice of what we add to our campus, our special
projects, and our leadership opportunities.

Perhaps you see students who are alone or who say they feel
invisible. Or maybe you're new to a school or just feel like you
don't fit in. In Psalm 142:4, King David says, "Look to the right
and see: there is none who takes notice of me; no refuge remains
to me; no one cares for my soul" (ESV). At some point in our
lives, we all feel that we could disappear and no one would notice.
God's loving eyes never overlook you though.

Step into conversations and greet people in the halls. Be a
friend. People notice how you make them feel. There are a lot
of lonely people in the world; don't wait for them to notice you.

Lord, prompt me to always acknowledge
those around me. Amen.

Bold Believers
and Willing Workers

Jesus was going through all the cities and villages. …
Seeing the people, He felt compassion for them, because
they were distressed and dispirited like sheep without a
shepherd. Then He said to His disciples, "The harvest
is plentiful, but the workers are few." –MATTHEW 9:35–37

God has sent you into the "fields" of education, where your influence is powerful and your opportunities are plentiful. Your workplace is your mission field. You are following Jesus' example. Wherever He was, He prayed, He cared, and He shared the message of God. He was never short on time, too busy to care, or too important to be compassionate.

Friends will bring people to you because of your reputation for prayer. Some will seek you out, and others will be grateful you approached them. Your life shows what it looks like to be a follower of Jesus Christ. Your school is filled with those who are "distressed and dispirited"; the New International Version calls them "helpless and harassed."

Jesus calls them the harvest, the ones He died for, and the reason He has you at this school—your mission field.

Jesus, I want to be a bold believer
and willing worker for you. Amen.

Led by Love

"The most important one," answered Jesus,
"is this: ... 'Love the Lord your God with all your heart
and with all your soul and with all your mind and with
all your strength.' The second is this: 'Love your neighbor
as yourself.' There is no commandment greater than these.'
" –MARK 12:29-31 NIV

In the Old Testament, God's people showed their love for Him by following the Law. When Jesus came, He taught that the greatest Law, which really summarized all the laws, was love. Jesus taught us to let love rule our lives.

What tends to steer your priorities? Time is precious and money is tight, family is a priority, and a career is necessary to provide money for your family. Rest is a basic need but somehow usually gets pushed to the bottom of our list. What about possessions? Where do they rank on your list?

None of these are inherently sinful; they just cannot be first in your life. Let everything you say and do be motivated by love: your love for God first and a godly love for others second. Then you will never go wrong.

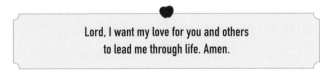

Lord, I want my love for you and others
to lead me through life. Amen.

United We Stand

And knowing their thoughts Jesus said to them,
"Any kingdom divided against itself is laid waste;
and any city or house divided against itself will not stand."
—MATTHEW 12:25

As members of the body of Christ, God calls us to unity in Him, yet division is a difficult subject that we have to deal with on an almost daily basis. Traditions, opinions, theology, philosophy, and personality all come into play in any relationship, workplace, church, or team.

It's important that educators share common goals and work in a collaborative environment. Communication, shared goals, and a dedicated heart for what is best for the student is a must if we are to be effective educators perpetuating successful students in a flourishing workplace. When we allow other motivations to take priority, our students suffer. Set the example of the staff strength through unity.

I tell you this not to bring you down, but to bring you together. Everyone agrees we need unity, but like most everything else, it won't happen without a plan. Consider today your plan to cultivate and protect unity with your fellow staff members, despite your differences.

Lord, give me wisdom so I can help
my school stand united. Amen.

Just

> So you shall observe to do *just* as the LORD your God
> has commanded you; … that you may live and that it
> may be well with you. –DEUTERONOMY 5:32–33

Today's verse tells us to do *just* as God commanded–nothing more, nothing less, completely and immediately. We have added other meanings such as "slightly," "merely," and "in a moment or so." I became aware of this while listening to students who were given instructions and did not follow them completely or in a timely manner. For example, they were told, "No talking," but they were "*Just* asking a question," "*Just* finishing a conversation," or "*Just* borrowing a pencil."

Somehow, they felt they were not disobeying at all because it was only a little bit. When told to go do something but I found them playing, they were "*just* seeing how far they could throw." They meant, "I was on my way, but I chose to do this first."

Has God given you instructions, but somehow, just like my students, you *just* had to do something else first? Lack of obedience is disobedience. We must not hesitate or deviate.

Lord, may I always obey you right away.
Amen.

The Goal of Our Instruction

But the goal of our instruction is love from a pure heart and a good conscience and a sincere faith. For some men, straying from these things, have turned aside to fruitless discussion, wanting to be teachers of the Law, even though they do not understand either what they are saying or the matters about which they make confident assertions.

–1 Timothy 1:5–7

The apostle Paul's goal for teaching was for others to learn and live love from a pure heart, a good conscience, and a sincere faith, because straying from these things leads to fruitless discussion and ill-equipped leadership. Without foundational values, there's a gap in the process of applying the subjects that students learn, leaving those subjects useless or dangerous.

What is the goal of your teaching? I'm sure you love to see students excel, but what is the biggest reason you became an educator? Was it to extend the knowledge of a particular subject, or did you want to change the world one student at a time? Ponder your reasons, and ask God to give you His perspective of each of your students. Pray for God's wisdom as you walk into your classroom each morning and ask God to show you how He would have you teach your students that day.

Lord, strengthen me to equip my students
to live a wise life through love. Amen.

Steady

> As long as Moses held up his hands, the Israelites
> were winning, but whenever he lowered his hands, the
> Amalekites were winning. When Moses' hands grew tired,
> they took a stone and put it under him and he sat on it.
> Aaron and Hur held his hands up—one on one side, one
> on the other—so that his hands remained steady till
> sunset. So Joshua overcame the Amalekite army with
> the sword.
> —EXODUS 17:11–13 NIV

Just as Hur and Aaron held up Moses' arms during the Amalekite battle "so that his hands remained steady" and to ensure victory for Joshua and Israel, the family of Jesus-followers must take turns lifting each other up in love, encouragement, deeds, and prayer.

Think of people who were on your side or by your side throughout a battle, how did they contribute to you and your victory? Thank God for them, and ask Him to show you someone who is in a battle and then go lift them up.

> Lord, may we as believers remain
> steady to victory together. Amen.

Help, Not Hinder

But Jesus said, "Let the little children come to me
and do not hinder them, for to such belongs the
kingdom of heaven." —MATTHEW 19:14 ESV

How can teachers help students encounter faith on campus? First, post information about students' opportunities to express and experience their faith. Events such as See You at the Pole and Christian clubs on their campus, as well as encouragement of expressing their faith in art, writings, and relationships, are just a few ways that students can exercise their faith.

Second, become a chaperone or sponsor for those who participate in prayer, service, studies, and clubs on campus. Sponsors provide classrooms and chaperones for meetings, give prayer covering, and are allowed to answer questions or give input when asked by students. We can also encourage students to research all of the great Christian student ministries that are available to meet the needs and vision of what they hope to see God accomplish at their school. Prepare in prayer, and be informed and ready to express the legality of these events and to protect students from bullying or threats imposed by their peers, staff, or even the administration.

Lord, let me exercise and experience faith
in you on my campus. Amen.

Every Nation, Tribe, and Tongue

> After this I looked, and there was a great multitude that
> no one could count, from every nation, from all tribes and
> peoples and languages, standing before the throne.
> —REVELATION 7:9 NRSV

Division and distrust are big problems in our nation that may
have spilled into your hallways and classroom. We are all
called to love our neighbors as ourselves, including the ones who
live in different neighborhoods, come from other nations, and
speak different languages. As a Christian of any color, ethnicity,
social, or financial background, we are called to love and to righteousness. Judgment and division have no place in the church.
We have to get our hearts right with God—all of us.

Jesus modeled what it meant to love one another with no exceptions. He stayed in Samaria, valued women and tax collectors,
healed people from other nations, and even healed the servant
of an enemy soldier. Jesus prayed that His followers would be
unified so that people would believe in Him. Let's be the answer
to His prayer.

Jesus, help me to always see the soul within and not
what's on the outside. We are your family. Amen.

Sharpened and Shaped

Iron sharpens iron, and one man sharpens another.
—PROVERBS 27:17 ESV

Interaction and nurturing between Christians is vital to our spiritual well-being. Just as iron rubbed against iron is shaped and sharpened, fellowship, prayer, Bible study, and other forms of worship with fellow Christians sharpen our character while shaping and strengthening our personal relationship with Jesus. This is important when it comes to finding Christian coworkers on campus; our prayers for one another, as well as encouragement and godly counsel, will help shape our school year and our reputation as an excellent educator.

Your actions, reactions, lessons, and love for your students will shape and sharpen your students as well. You help mold the minds and hearts as well as the priorities and future decisions of your students. You give them an educational foundation, but your character will teach them to love learning or at least love the subject you teach. Your influence rubs away the rough edges and equips them for the days and years ahead.

> Lord, guide me to make contact with those who will sharpen and shape me, and with those I can shape and sharpen. Amen.

Knowing Who You Really Are

> But you are a chosen race, a royal priesthood, a holy
> nation, a people for God's own possession, so that you may
> proclaim the excellencies of Him who has called you out
> of darkness into His marvelous light. —1 PETER 2:9

In the education world, we try our best to avoid labeling our students. The word *label* comes with many negative connotations, but if it weren't for labels, we wouldn't know what was in the cans and boxes sitting on our pantry shelves. Labels voice value that we can't see from the outside.

Finish this sentence with a word (other than your name) that would label you or help describe who you are: I am _____.

How did you choose your label today, and what factored into your decision? Were you serious or silly? Do the things you say about yourself agree or dispute with God's labels on you? Now think about how your students might finish this sentence. How they label themselves may be very revealing, and it will certainly help direct your prayers for them.

> Lord, align my label with who you say I am.
> Amen.

Saved

For with the heart one believes and is justified, and with the mouth one confesses and is saved. —ROMANS 10:10 ESV

Are you a Christian? I have been writing to you, assuming you are, but are you a Bible-believing, sin-confessing, forgiven-by-the-blood-of-Jesus Christ-follower? I'm not asking you if you attend church. I'm not asking, "If you died tonight, where would you want to go?"

Salvation is *not* a death destination decision; I don't know too many people who would pick hell over heaven as their eternal destination. The question you're deciding is who you want to live for. God gave you life and has great plans for you, but He will not bless your nonsense. It is impossible for us to fix our sin problem; we cannot get the most out of life and go to heaven on our own. The best life begins when we ask Him to be our Lord and Savior. This is not a get-out-of-hell-free card; it is a commitment to love Him and live your life for His glory, through His power and plan.

> Jesus, I confess you as my Lord,
> today and always. Amen.

Lesson Plan for Life

May he give you the desire of your heart
and make all your plans succeed. —PSALM 20:4 NIV

Imagine giving your students an assignment and telling them to turn it in whenever. When do you think they would turn it in? Tomorrow, two weeks from now, or maybe never? This is why we use techniques and tools to check off our to-do list. By making a list of what we need to do and prioritizing items by importance, we ensure that things get done.

These techniques should sound familiar to us as teachers as well. They're how we fill our lesson plan book with daily, weekly, and semester instructions. Success does not happen haphazardly; progress and success require an intentional strategic plan. We cannot just hope our students will learn all the state-required standards and life skills they need to progress and be successful in the next grade and in life. Deadlines and assessments throughout the process help us to stay on track to hit the target.

We all need a lesson plan for life. Live intentionally, or time will have a way of flying by like summertime.

Lord, help me to write and live
a lesson plan for life. Amen.

October

Awaken with Wisdom

"The Sovereign LORD has given me his words of wisdom,
so that I know how to comfort the weary.
Morning by morning he wakens me and opens
my understanding to his will." —ISAIAH 50:4 NLT

The call to be an educator keeps us on our knees and under God's wings for strength, wisdom, and patience. It is an awesome and sometimes overwhelming task that can keep us awake at night praying for our students and all that needs to be accomplished in our classroom and in their lives. In my teaching career, there were many nights that I went to bed feeling defeated and ready to quit, but when morning came, God had restored my strength and perseverance.

How about you? Do you ever feel like you're in over your head? Have you ever reconsidered your career in October, thinking there's no way you'll make it to May? Maybe you have a student or even a whole class that is challenging you beyond anything you've experienced in years before. If so, receive Christ's wisdom to instruct and inspire you when you are weary.

Lord, waken me each morning with words
of wisdom to do your will. Amen.

Bullying

Set a guard over my mouth, Lord;
keep watch over the door of my lips. –Psalm 141:3 niv

Some people feel powerful when they exert excessive or abusive authority, whether it is physically or emotionally. We call it bullying, and this type of behavior is actually a cry of insecurity, sometimes because the person has been the victim of bullying. While we cannot in any way condone or comprehend the actions of school shooters, we know that being bullied often feeds their hatred for their school and the students they target.

Think of a time when you have felt insecure, embarrassed, regretful, or not accepted. What did you do in these situations? Did you make compromises that you later regretted? Have you ever made someone else look dumb or weak in order to get a laugh, affirmation, or attention?

Bullying is not just a student issue. People are bullied at all ages, by people of all ages. Some teachers have been bullied by students, parents, and their administrators. Being bullied is a serious issue, and I encourage you to reach out for help if you are a victim.

Jesus, please guard me so I never participate in
or put up with bullying. Amen.

Do Not Fear

"When you pass through the waters, I will be with you;
and through the rivers, they will not overflow you.
When you walk through the fire, you will not be scorched,
nor will the flame burn you." –ISAIAH 43:2

What would you do if your worst fear came true? Mine did in October 2009.

Chandler, my son, complained about pain in his face so severe that he couldn't chew his food. We took him for tests and received a diagnosis of Langerhans cell histiocytosis. This began a cancer journey that meant hundreds of doctor and hospital visits, scans, labs, oxygen, and chemo.

It's impossible to prepare for our worst fear coming to pass, but we have an awesome God! He surprises us with strength and peace that we never thought we could experience, even when we're living our worst nightmare.

Maybe you're living your worst fears come true, or have walked "through the fire" and have your own story to tell. How do you manage such difficulties? I can only tell you what I did: Trust, one breath at a time.

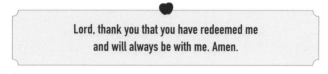

Lord, thank you that you have redeemed me
and will always be with me. Amen.

Practicing Fear

The fear of the LORD is the beginning of wisdom;
a good understanding have all those who practice it.
His praise endures forever! –PSALM 111: 10 RSV

As Halloween décor fills our stores, schools, and lawns, it strikes fear in the hearts of some and triggers delight in others. Some focus on the scare, while others focus on the sweets, tricks, and treats.

The fear of the Lord brings its own sweet reward. It is a respecting fear, not a run-away type fear. It means to acknowledge awesomeness and to be struck with terror at the thought of disobedience—a faithful fear.

Can you think of a time when you had to risk man's vengeance in obedience to God's commands? Perhaps you feared you would lose your job if you lived out your faith at school. We must stand up for our religious rights, but we don't want to go looking for a fight. In situations where you must make a righteous stand, be wise and fear the Lord.

> Lord, may I always practice the fear of you.
> Amen.

Applying Ourselves

And let our people learn to apply themselves to good deeds,
so as to help cases of urgent need, and not be unfruitful.
–TITUS 3:14 ESV

As educators, it is so frustrating for us to see someone fail to reach their potential. We search for the button to push that will jump-start them to apply the abilities we know they possess but haven't been motivated to utilize.

Think about what causes people to settle for less than they could accomplish. Apprehension of the unknown, laziness, fear of failure, or sometimes just not knowing the right steps to take may hold people back. So how do we help a student reach potential?

Experiencing a taste of success brings incredible motivation. For the competitive type, a good competition will spark a flame. For those who like to please, an "I'm so proud of you" will go a long way. The challenge of finding the secret to motivating a classroom, or several classrooms full of students, can be overwhelming. Pray over them and ask God to show you what will inspire them.

Lord, help me and my students to apply ourselves fully to
"help cases of urgent need, and not be unfruitful." Amen.

Fire Prevention Week

And have mercy on some, who are doubting;
save others, snatching them out of the fire. –JUDE 2–23

In the United States, the second full week of October is National Fire Prevention Week. Its purpose is to increase the awareness of fire's dangers and to educate people on how to stay safe from fire.

There is also a style of preaching the gospel called "fire and brimstone." It harshly focuses on the perils of hell, calling on sinners to repent and be saved from the flames that await them. While I fully believe in hell and all the Bible teaches about it, I have never embraced this style of evangelism. I believe most people are more repulsed by this style, responding better to the invitation of heaven rather than running from the warning of hell. But perhaps there are some who do need the dire warning so that they turn to God.

Regardless of style, we must pray for our students, during this Fire Prevention Week and at all times, that by whatever means necessary they are snatched from the fires of hell.

> Lord, thank you that with your help I can make
> every week Fire Prevention Week. Amen.

Eagerly Extol Every Day

I will extol You, my God, O King, and I will bless Your name forever and ever. Every day I will bless You, and I will praise Your name forever and ever. –PSALM 145:1–2

We need to bless God, praise Him, and speak of His glory, knowing that He is near as we call upon Him. I challenge you to eagerly extol Him every day with heartfelt and enthusiastic praise and thanks. Note how it changes your heart, your mood, and your day. It is good for your attitude to be filled with gratitude.

Because the church is made up of humans, we must be careful not to be a grumbling and discouraged group. We cannot watch God "move mountains" one day and be downcast with doubt the next. The cure for being downcast is to look up and speak up in praise and worship. Get excited and energetic in your time of thanks to the Lord.

Lord, may my voice fill the heavens and the earth as I eagerly extol you every day. Amen.

Divine Desires

May he grant you your heart's desire and
fulfill all your plans! —PSALM 20:4 ESV

What do you desire? Pause and think that over for a minute. Do you have time to think about the things you *want* to do, or are you just overwhelmed with the things you *have* to do?

I once reached a point in my life when I felt like my schedule, commitments, urgent situations, and interruptions were running my life. My days were full, almost frantic, but eighteen hours later I would lie awake wondering what I had accomplished.

Plans, goals, and boundaries are essential. Learn what to say no to and set a course for a clearer vision of what God is calling you to do—and not do. Stop, pray, regroup, reorganize, prioritize, and open your heart and mind to big dreams. God has given you gifts, strengths, and interests, and He has a divine plan for your life. If you don't have any idea what you really desire, ask Him to give you divine dreams, to put His glorifying desires in your heart.

> Lord, open my mind and time to the desires
> that will flood my heart and give you glory. Amen.

Helped by Prayer

You also must help us by prayer, so that many will give
thanks on our behalf for the blessing granted us through
the prayers of many. –2 CORINTHIANS 1:11 ESV

Prayer is powerful, bringing us into the presence of God who
provides for all His plans and people. Our prayers reflect our
love for Him and the people created in His image. It is important
that we share our prayer requests with other people so they can
be petitioning heaven for us, our schools, and our students.

Do you have an intercessory team that prays for you daily?
If so, ask them to pray that an epidemic of Christ's love will be
expressed and experienced on every campus. Imagine what it will
look like when God answers that prayer, and let it be an inspirit-
ing vision that motivates all that you do, say, and pray. Jesus, the
model Teacher, not only gave instruction but also met people's
physical, emotional, and spiritual needs. Pray for campuses that
must spend most of their money and motivation caring and coun-
seling, and pray provision for more time and energy to focus on
curriculum.

> Lord, please supply all that we need to fulfill
> your will on every campus. Amen.

Children of the Most High

> But love your enemies, do good to them … and you will
> be children of the Most High, because he is kind to the
> ungrateful and wicked. –LUKE 6:35 NIV

One October, my daughter, Emily, and I headed into a store behind an adorable little girl. As we stepped through the doors, a large mechanical witch began to shriek and move her arms and long, twisted fingers. Emily tried to run between the witch and the little girl to keep her from being scared, but it was too late.

The little girl stood staring at the witch for a moment, then walked right up to it and hugged it! The mechanical witch continued to squirm and screech, but the little girl held on tight, refusing to let go. Her mother finally pulled her away, and with a final kiss on the witch's cheek, she smiled and waved goodbye.

How kind are we to people who are ungrateful or wicked? The witch seemed unlovable to us. She was made to scare, but the child had been taught to care. May we do the same.

> Lord, let my love show that I am your child.
> Amen.

Meeting the Needs, Sowing the Seeds

For I was hungry and you gave me food, I was thirsty and
you gave me drink, I was a stranger and you welcomed me.
—MATTHEW 25:35 ESV

There are people, churches, and ministries in your community
that focus on serving schools. Some are willing to fill backpacks with school supplies, while others set up coat drives to keep
students warm in the winter. If you need faithful volunteers to
help meet your day-in-and-day-out needs or for bigger projects,
consider asking your church and a few others close to your school
to consider "adopting" your school. Members could tutor, help
with Christian clubs, in the classroom and school, raise funding,
and collect food and other necessities for families in need.

Pray for your helpers, and pray that there will be Christian
prayer groups and student-led clubs on every campus. Pray for
all school buildings to be safe and clean, and for after-school
programs to be provided so that children are safe and taught
character and skills that will help them to grow and reach their
God-given purpose.

Lord, I ask you to meet our needs, and I thank you
for those who serve and sow the seeds of your love
on our campus and in our district. Amen.

Discovering the Dream, and the Voyage of a Vision

Your old men will dream dreams,
your young men will see visions. –JOEL 2:28

Beyond today or even this year, what do your students want to accomplish?

It has been reported that this generation is different from the past several generations; they are less focused on material wealth and think more about making a difference in the world. They want to care for the downtrodden, and they value getting a job where they can use their skills to help others and serve the hurting and helpless. Unlike previous generations, they are less fixated on having "bigger and better" than their parents.

How can you help them make their dreams a reality? How do you persuade them on the path that they should go, and encourage them not to depart from it? Pray God's presence and power over them. Pray that God would fill their minds with His plan for their lives and that they will serve in His name. Pray that they will spread His message as well as His love.

> Lord, give me wisdom to help others discover their dreams and map out the voyage to the visions you give them. Amen.

Find or Be Found

If you search for good, you will find favor;
but if you search for evil, it will find you! –Proverbs 11:27 NLT

After a rough morning, do you find yourself thinking, *It's going to be one of those days*, only to have things go from bad to worse? Did you ever stop to think that it was because you were expecting bad things and started watching for them? Now think about what you look for in a new staff member or student who you have heard bad things about. Do you immediately start looking for the good in them to dispel the negative reputation?

Scripture says we will find what we focus on. Looking for God's best in a day, circumstance, or person will be our guide to find it. If you search for evil, it will be a short search; evil is waiting to make an appearance at the first idea of your attention. Search for good and for God in every encounter. Look for opportunities to show love and faith and be the good someone else is searching for in this world.

> Jesus, you are good, and I set my sights on
> seeing you throughout my days. Amen.

Filled to Fulfill

"Look, I have chosen Bezalel son of Uri, grandson of Hur,
of the tribe of Judah. I have filled him with the Spirit of
God, giving him great wisdom, ability, and expertise
in all kinds of crafts." –EXODUS 31:2-3 NLT

Bezalel was the man responsible for building the Ark of the
Covenant and other articles for the tabernacle (Exodus 37:1–
11). If God had simply said, "I command you to do this," Bezalel
might have crumbled under the pressure of overwhelming responsibilities. It's not like he could Google "Ark of the Covenant"
and pull up instructions and diagrams on how to build it. No,
Bezalel had something much better than Google; he was filled
with the Spirit of God, who gave him all the wisdom, ability, and
expertise needed to fulfill his calling.

You have been chosen by God to be an educator. As a Christian, you are indwelled with the Holy Spirit, and when you yield
to Him, He fills you. God is still the giver of intelligence, skill,
knowledge, wisdom, and instructions. He only requires us to
yield and be filled to fulfill His will.

> Lord, fill me with your Spirit to fulfill your will.
> Amen.

Protect and Preserve

Protect me, for I am devoted to you. Save me,
for I serve you and trust you. You are my God.
—Psalm 86:2 NLT

Think about your first response when you see a police officer.
Do you check your speed, or do you feel safe knowing the officer is there for your protection? Are you a law abider or bender?
Now think about your students: how does their respect for your
rules and enjoyment of your class make you feel?

Police work to protect and serve, and God promises to protect
and preserve us if we are devoted to obeying and serving Him.
If we could physically see God on the road, we could do a quick
life check through prayer every day, by asking Him to show us
anything that does not please Him. This prayer practice presents
our devotion to God and gives us a strong sense of peace and
protection knowing that He is preserving us.

Students want safety in their classrooms and schools. Are you
good at recognizing when to intervene? Are you good at spotting
rule-breakers? And how can you earn respect and trust?

Lord, please protect me.
I am devoted to serve you. Amen.

Praying for Light in the Dark

For God so loved the world, that He gave His only begotten Son, that whoever believes in Him shall not perish, but have eternal life. For God did not send the Son into the world to judge the world, but that the world might be saved through Him. –John 3:16–17

The entertainment industry shapes culture, influencing how the world thinks, feels, lives, and even loves. We see the spiritual battle as it attempts to replace God with fame, fortune, and financial abundance, and it affects even the youngest of our students.

An estimated 2 percent of the arts and entertainment industry are Christian. Tragically, there is so much hate mail sent to Christians trying to work in the darkness of Hollywood. But we cannot expect those who do not know Jesus to behave like Christians. How will they know about God's love if we don't go with compassion, instead of criticism, and tell them—or, better yet, show it?

Pray for the entertainment industry—that those who love the Lord will continue to stand up for their beliefs amid the criticism they receive, and that those who don't know Him will have their lives touched by believers in a life-changing way. Shining the light of Jesus in Hollywood will shine His light on our culture.

Lord, give me a love for the entertainment industry. I pray they will know you as their Lord. Amen.

Saved (or Stolen) by the Bell

> Blessed is the one who finds wisdom, and the one
> who gets understanding, for the gain from her is better
> than gain from silver and her profit better than gold.
> —PROVERBS 3:13–14 ESV

You've probably heard the phrase, "Saved by the bell!" It's usually a victory cry or a shout of relief that the bell sounded before the teacher could give consequences to a disobedient student, a quiz to a distracted class, or homework to a disruptive class. The teacher had been aptly prepared and capable of fulfilling all that was planned for the day, but disturbances continually diverted the flow of time and teaching. Then, all of a sudden, time was up and the bell rang. Learning would have advanced, a quiz would have given insight into their comprehension, and homework would have provided practice leading to proficiency … if time hadn't ran out.

But as the students fled the classroom thinking they were victorious, the teacher was left feeling the loss of all that could have been gained, and skills that result in success were delayed for another day. In reality, no one won that day.

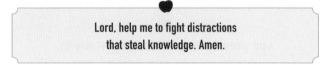

Lord, help me to fight distractions
that steal knowledge. Amen.

The Three Rs

Pay to all what is owed: … respect to whom respect is owed,
honor to whom honor is owed. –ROMANS 13:7 ESV

Like the foundational three Rs of school, we have the three Rs of our family. The first R is "respectful." We ask ourselves, "Am I being respectful to God, the person I am speaking with, and authority?" The second R is "responsible." We ask, "Am I being responsible with what I have been given, with what I have been asked to do, and with what needs to be done?" The final R is "represent." In all that we do and say, we ask ourselves, "Am I representing God, my family, and myself in a positive way?" If the answer to any of these questions is no, then we need to repent.

These Rs are short enough to remember and simple enough to apply to every situation. Consider using them in your classroom and your life. Just imagine what life would look like if we all lived by these three Rs.

Lord, let these three Rs resonate richly in my life.
Amen.

Filled with Good Things

Let them give thanks to the LORD for his unfailing love and his wonderful deeds for men, for he satisfies the thirsty and fills the hungry with good things. —PSALM 107:8–9 NIV

If you're feeling a little empty today, I pray these verses will help fill you with gladness and gratefulness. When I struggle to search for a positive thought, I take an account of how my life is filled with so many good things, because God's heart toward us is displayed in His actions when we hunger for Him and refuse to have an appetite for the things of this world.

Psalm 107 follows this pattern: The people did _____ (rebellious or disobedient act). The consequential disaster that followed was _____. The people cried out to God and repented. God blessed them with _____, and they responded by giving Him enthusiastic thanks.

Now think about how you could personally fill in these blanks. What has happened in your lifetime that mirrors the verses of this chapter?

> Lord, I thank you for your unfailing love and wonderful deeds.
> I will testify that you satisfy the thirsty and fill the
> hungry with good things. Amen.

Called to Give Hope

I pray that your hearts will be flooded with light so that you can understand the confident hope he has given to those he called—his holy people who are his rich and glorious inheritance. I also pray that you will understand the incredible greatness of God's power for us who believe him. This is the same mighty power that raised Christ from the dead. —EPHESIANS 1:18–20 NLT

Real hope is powerful. You have students dealing with immense weights: drama at home and in school, divorced parents, financial hardships, and sick loved ones. We *all* need hope.

Hope is our Savior, who hears prayers and sets answers in motion. Hope is sensitive and steadfast—a heart that is brave enough to love compassionately and bold enough to run at a giant with a slingshot and a prayer. Hope moves us to drink Christ's living water and overcome a thirst for culture. And God has called *you* to be a dispenser of hope.

Teachers and coaches rank as the top two influencers in testimonies of people who overcome great adversity. You touch the present and impact the future.

Lord, may the flood of your hope in my heart overflow and reach everyone around me. Amen.

Zealous

Never be lacking in zeal, but keep your spiritual fervor,
serving the Lord. –ROMANS 12:11 NIV

The New Living Translation of this verse says, "Don't be lazy, but work hard and serve the Lord enthusiastically." I had to chuckle at this because *lazy* is definitely not a characteristic of a successful educator; we stay busy night and day, working far more hours than many people imagine. *Zeal* means passion, warmth, earnestness, and fire. It takes lots of prayer and perseverance to work at a teacher's pace with increasing energy and enthusiasm.

Do you know someone who never seems to run out of zeal? They're the kind of people we enjoy being in a room with, and we feed off their fire. They light up a room when they walk in, and if they're an educator, their class is energized and engaged; students even hang out there.

Perhaps I'm describing you. Your passion affects your co-workers and students; they look forward to spending time with you. Let your zeal continue to be charged by your love for serving Jesus.

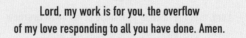

Lord, my work is for you, the overflow
of my love responding to all you have done. Amen.

Sealed Lips

A gossip goes about telling secrets,
but one who is trustworthy in spirit keeps a confidence.
—PROVERBS 11:13 NRSV

Gossip. This one word can stir up so many thoughts and emotions. If you've been the victim of gossip, you know that the pain is indescribable. Why do lies seem to travel faster than truth? Sometimes intended information is really rumors spread as, "So-and-so said …," but the source's trustworthiness goes down the drain as the truth unfolds. We see our students spread gossip and fall victim to it, sometimes all in the same day.

As educators, we need to gather pertinent information to resolve problems. Pray that God would prick your heart and seal your lips if at any point your search for truth turns to gossip. Here are some questions to ask yourself when you wonder, *Am I gossiping?*:

- Am I just curious or sincerely concerned?
- Am I willing and working to be part of the solution?
- Have I prayed over this situation and information? If someone shared this information about me, how would I feel?
- Am I saying this for righteousness or revenge?

Your answers will make the answer clear.

**Lord, may gossip stay far away from me.
Amen.**

Come with Authority

"Now have come the salvation and the power and the
kingdom of our God, and the authority of his Messiah.
For the accuser of our brothers and sisters …
has been hurled down." –REVELATION 12:10 NIV

I must warn you at this point that satan is less than thrilled that
you are praying every day and glorifying God at your school.
Here are a few popular schemes that he hopes you will fall for, as
well as a battle plan:

- *I don't have time to pray today. There are so many other things I
  need to get done.* View prayer as having an appointment
  with God Himself. He will always be the first one
  there, and He never misses a meeting.
- *No one wants to hear my problems and prayer requests. Everyone
  has their own problems.* Yes, we all have burdens and trials,
  but God gave us fellow sojourners to lift us up when
  we get down.
- *I really cannot trust people. This school runs on gossip, and I will
  just be the next juicy morsel.* Pray that the "Have you heard
  …?" hotline will be disconnected.
- *I'll just skip this one time.* Don't. It becomes a habit.

Lord, may I pray with the authority of Christ,
and may the accuser not report me absent. Amen.

Responsive

> "Worthy are you, our Lord and God, to receive glory and honor and power, for you created all things, and by your will they existed and were created." –REVELATION 4:11 ESV

As educators, we expect students (and hopefully parents) to respond to our authority and affection. When we give instructions, they should be followed; when we give a deadline, it should be met. And when we express grace by extending the date a paper or project is due or give the opportunity to retake a quiz, we expect appreciation. We hope students will respond to their second chance and new opportunity with their full attention and application.

Sadly, we have all probably experienced the pain of disrespect or even being duped. How do you respond when you are disrespected or deceived? Does your heart harden, making you deny mercy to the next student who asks for it? Just remember that we are to give grace, just as God does. Compare this with your response to Christ's authority and affection and pause to give Him the honor and glory that He is worthy to receive.

> Lord, may my response to you reflect my affection and appreciation. Amen.

Turn Worry to Worship

Don't worry about anything; instead, pray about
everything. Tell God what you need, and thank him for all
he has done. —Philippians 4:6 nlt

What's on your mind right now? Are you thinking about work, bills, family, or your to-do list that never seems to get any shorter? Perhaps there are things going on at your school— relationships in trouble, students you're concerned about, or deadlines that seemed months away and are now just days away. Instead of letting them distract you during your devotional time, turn your worries into worship.

God wants you to talk with Him about everything on your heart and mind. Turn these distractions into prayer prompts; you can pray about everything. Maybe you were just thinking about what to cook for dinner; stop and thank Him for food. Remind yourself that if it is worth pondering, then it is worth prayer.

Change begins when your knees bend. If you are prone to distraction or worry, know that prayer invites God into your circumstances and change begins when you call on Him.

> Lord, I know it is a waste to worry, and so I worship
> you now in prayer and thanksgiving. Amen.

Testify

But I do not account my life of any value nor as precious
to myself, if only I may finish my course and the ministry
that I received from the Lord Jesus, to testify to the
gospel of the grace of God. –ACTS 20:24 ESV

Sharing your personal testimony is an important part of a
Christian's life and is obeying Christ's command to go and
make disciples. I would like to challenge you to write your testimony. Here are my suggestions to get you started. Write down:

1. The trial you went through
2. How you reacted at first in relation to God
3. Was your struggle a result of sin or not
4. Who ministered to you and how
5. How God transformed you
6. If you had a favorite Scripture during the time
7. How your struggle was resolved, or is still being resolved
8. How you have been changed
9. Who Jesus is to you and what role He plays in your life

God will give you an opportunity to share someday. It is up
to you to prepare.

> Lord, I want to testify to the great things you have done.
> Please help me prepare to share our story. Amen.

Fear Factor

"Are not five sparrows sold for two cents?
Yet not one of them is forgotten before God. Indeed,
the very hairs of your head are all numbered. Do not fear;
you are more valuable than many sparrows." –LUKE 12:6–7

Fear can be a terrible stronghold in a person's life. It is actually the opposite of faith. When we operate in fear, we tell God that He is not trustworthy enough—and that somehow the thing we fear is bigger than He is. When we read it that way, fear really doesn't make a whole lot of sense, does it?

Faith magnifies God and activates His Spirit in us. Fear holds us captive, but faith catapults us into amazing opportunities to achieve our dreams. Fear keeps us from trying, but faith perseveres. Fear manipulates, but faith motivates. Fear steals, but faith reveals. Faith allows God access to every area of our lives. Faith is strengthened in prayer and with fellowship of other Christians. Faith does not analyze God, it obeys.

Now, what do you fear? Absolutely nothing!

Lord, thank you for setting me free from fear.
Amen.

Spiritual Standards

All the people answered together and said,
"All that the LORD has spoken we will do!" –EXODUS 19:8

All of us operate under various sets of standards. Schools set dress standards, discipline standards, and so on. Unfortunately, we often see students pushing the limits, if not disregarding them altogether. To help prevent this from happening, put the *stand* in *standards* early in the school year by setting the standard of excellence at your school.

God has set spiritual standards for His people. It is important to remember that they are for us, His followers, and that is where accountability begins. We cannot slack off on God's standards; they're meant to protect and provide for us. We find covering and comfort in them, and they strengthen and sustain us. Just think about how a world of unbelievers would respond to Christians who lack obedience to the mighty God we say we serve.

God calls us to be holy, separated from the world for His name's sake. We can see disobedience so clearly in our students, and today we must pray that God opens our eyes so we can see it in ourselves.

Lord, I desire to hear, see, and adhere
to scriptural spiritual standards. Amen.

Interrupted

Then Jesus entered a house, and again a crowd gathered,
so that he and his disciples were not even able to eat.
—MARK 3:20 NIV

As adults, my kids still visit teachers from their school years. I'm sure it's an interruption since many teachers often give up eating to get things done, but I pray that as a teacher, you stop to soak up the appreciation and admiration of students from previous years.

In Jesus' short time on earth, crowds followed Him everywhere. He taught them, had compassion on them, touched their hearts, healed their hurts, and changed their lives. As a result, people chased Him, touched Him, interrupted His meals, and even cut open roofs to get to Him. From time to time, He and the disciples had to withdraw, but when the children came, He took the children in His arms, put His hands on them, and blessed them.

You are adored. You are admired. You have taught, touched hearts, and changed lives. Some of your students may be fanatic admirers. I pray they never cut through your roof, but I hope you will enjoy their love.

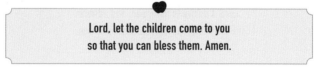

Lord, let the children come to you
so that you can bless them. Amen.

Speaking to a Friend

The LORD would speak to Moses face to face,
as one speaks to a friend. —EXODUS 33:11 NIV

I was with a friend, and her phone kept ringing. "Aren't you going to answer that?" I asked. She said no, explaining that the caller was a "friend" who only called when she needed something. She called to borrow things, ask for childcare, or ask for help when she overcommitted herself. She also called for advice but rarely took it, instead making a big mess of things and then wanting others to clean it up. She never called to say thank you or to invite my friend to lunch. In fact, she never offered to do anything in return. "I want a friendship, but she seems to think I'm just here to tend to all her needs," my friend finished.

That situation made me think of how we treat Jesus sometimes. We pray when we need something—when we are out of ideas, resources, and energy—but then sometimes forget to call back and say thank you. Jesus desires a closeness that shares everything and talks often, not just when we need something. Today and in the days to come, make a point to spend time with Him just because you love Him.

Jesus, I want to live out a friendship with you.
Amen.

From Spooky to Spirit-Filled

"Thus says the LORD God to these bones, 'Behold, I will cause breath to enter you that you may come to life. I will put sinews on you, make flesh grow back on you, cover you with skin and put breath in you that you may come alive; and you will know that I am the LORD.'" —EZEKIEL 37:5–6

I'm not a big fan of Halloween, but I'm also not a protester of it. I love seeing children all dressed up in a parade or trick-or-treating at my door. I say a prayer for each child as I drop treats in their bags and buckets.

This Halloween, see it as an opportunity to pray—a lot! Take things that satan has set apart for evil and reclaim them in the name of Jesus for kingdom purposes. Likewise, I commission you today to pray every time you see a skeleton or gravestone decoration during Halloween season, that those who are still skeletons in need of God's Spirit in them will be brought from death to life.

> Lord, may I pray the spooky into Spirit-filled,
> and the gory into glory. Amen.

November

If

If my people, who are called by my name, will humble themselves and pray and seek my face and turn from their wicked ways, then will I hear from heaven and will forgive their sin and will heal their land. —2 CHRONICLES 7:14 NIV

It's sometimes difficult for me to ask educators to pray for our nation without getting political. Part of this is because educators are such a diverse group with differing opinions and preferences among them.

One year, as I prayed over the election, God helped bring clarity to this issue. He told me I should be praying over the church, that we would collectively address our own issues instead of judging the world for theirs. I knew I was guilty of this, being too busy beating the lost over the head with my biblical beliefs rather than living a loving life of faith that reaches out to them and expresses truth in love.

When we lay down our opinions to humble ourselves to pray, it refocuses us on what matters most—love—and invites God to come heal our land.

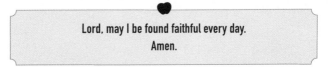

Lord, may I be found faithful every day.
Amen.

Vote and Pray beyond Election Day

Obey your leaders and submit to them. … Let them
do this with joy and not with groaning, for that would be
of no advantage to you. –HEBREWS 13:17 ESV

As voters in a democracy, we want to know what our elected officials believe, what they value, and what forms their character. We would like to think that they would publicly express and live out their beliefs, since psychologists say that we behave as we believe. What a concept! So if we profess Christian beliefs, our outward public expression should show that.

Voting for school board members all the way up to the president of the United States is one of the most important public expressions of your private beliefs, but it does not end on Election Day, because that is where the voting of those we elect begins. We must pray for our elected officials, show up at meetings, and send e-mails to encourage them to lead and vote their professed biblical worldview. Participate and pray every day so their service is joyful; it is your chance to make a difference.

> Lord, may the officials we elect make godly
> decisions for our schools. Amen.

Achoo!

Dear friend, I pray that you may enjoy good health
and that all may go well with you, even as your soul
is getting along well. –3 JOHN 1:2 NIV

Our usual response when someone sneezes is, "God bless you!" Blessing those who sneeze is an ancient tradition across many cultures, rooted in the belief that it helps protect from disease, evil spirits, and death. Today we must continue blessing others in the face of illness.

Healthcare is a God-sent blessing, yet it is inaccessible to some. Even so, prayer is accessible to all. As educators, we have a responsibility to pray for and bless our students regarding far more than protection from germs and bacteria. We should also be praying for protection from drugs, alcohol abuse, premarital sex, cutting, bullying, using their bodies to get attention, unhealthy relationships, and much more.

Your blessing is a powerful influence over all these things. Stay encouraged and keep praying for your students. You are making a huge difference!

Lord, please bless my students so that they can
enjoy good health and protection from evil. Amen.

Growing Gradually Greater Glory

And again He said, "To what shall I compare
the kingdom of God? It is like leaven, which a woman took
and hid in three pecks of flour until it was all leavened."
—LUKE 13:20–21

Jesus presents the idea of about fifty pounds of flour that is permeated and transformed by a pinch of yeast. That is our mission at our schools and in our communities. As Christ-followers, we are supposed to permeate our culture with the love and message of Jesus. We may feel small and insignificant, but that is exactly Jesus' point; even the smallest of seeds, when sown by the hand of Jesus, will have supernatural Spirit-filled success.

You may feel small and insignificant, but you make a big difference at your school. Think about what you would like to accomplish in or around it. The needs around you are great. Consider helping to feed the free-lunch students over the holidays and during the summer, or working to increase English learning skills in the areas that need it most. Maybe you feel called to host a Bible club at your home or church, or to go on a mission trip. Pray about what God would have you do and then act.

Lord, help me to realize my full growth potential.
May your kingdom grow in me and through me,
for your greater glory. Amen.

Driven to Succeed

Then, because so many people were coming and going
that they did not even have a chance to eat, he said to them,
"Come with me by yourselves to a quiet place and
get some rest." –MARK 6:31 NIV

One of the requirements in a parent's job description seems to be "professional driver." And when activities run back to back or overlap, moms and dads may have to become racecar drivers. After all, if we want our children to be successful, they have to be "driven." (Sorry–just a little joke.)

What do you think is the average bedtime of your students? While it's important to be involved and to exercise the talents God has given us, sometimes we can compromise quality for quantity in the search for success. Realize that many of your students are "driven to succeed" every night, every week, every season of the year. Sports, school activities, church, scouts, clubs, and music lessons all add up, and somewhere in there we mix in homework, chores, or even a job, and hopefully sleep.

What about you and your family? How many meals do you eat in the car each week? What time do you get to bed? What could you do to increase the time you have to rest?

Lord, may I find time to rest in
my pursuit for success. Amen.

Know It and Show It

"How great you are, O Sovereign LORD! There is no one like you, and there is no God but you, as we have heard with our own ears." —2 SAMUEL 7:22 NIV

How great is your God? What is bigger than Him? What is He incapable of doing? Take a few moments to think about these questions.

I hope that in your meditation, you reflected deeply on our all-powerful, all-knowing, ever-loving God, because this leads me to another question: Are you living your life as if you're a loved and protected child of this all-powerful, amazing God?

When God asks me to do something but I don't do it, I have to ask myself, "Do I not trust the One who knows and sees everything past, present, and future?" The way we live is really what we believe. I can tell you that I believe I'm a fish, but unless I grow gills and scales and look and live like a fish, it doesn't matter what I say I believe.

So let me ask you again: How great is our God?

Lord, thank you that I can trust you
to be great on my behalf. Amen.

Distracted

Mary … sat at the Lord's feet and listened to his teaching. But Martha was distracted with much. –LUKE 10:39–40 ESV

Perhaps one of the biggest frustrations of an educator is trying to pour wisdom, knowledge, and understanding into a generation that is filled with entertainment, extracurricular activities, and electronic devices. It is challenging to hold their attention for a fifty-minute class period, much less have them attend to all that they need to read and do in order to reach their full potential and godly purpose.

Do you see a culture that seeks to be entertained rather than to exert the energy it takes to be successful? How well do they focus? Is it possible to read and retain information while breaking to text every few minutes? And how do we grasp and teach the necessary affection, attention, and action it takes to truly be victorious?

Think about the enemy's ploys to distract our culture from recognizing the need for and following the lead of Jesus. What are some ways you can counter this?

Lord, you created us to reach our intellectual potential by focusing. Help me and my students to put away distractions. Amen.

Keep Your Commitments

Commit your way to the LORD; trust in him
and he will do this: He will make your righteousness
shine like the dawn, your vindication like the noonday sun.
—PSALM 37:5–6 NIV

Years ago, I was responsible for finding workers for a booth for a school event. When I called parents and asked them to help, they said they would "drop in" or would "visit and help for a while." But I needed commitments, not visitors. Have you ever been in a situation like that? Maybe you've had people promise to help with a special project in your classroom or on a field trip, but they didn't show up.

God calls you to commitments too—to sign up and show up and shine in His name. He commits to bless everything you commit to Him. Know that you can count on God's every Scripture and every promise. He will never let you down, get a better offer, forget, or decide He is just too tired.

Lord, I commit my ways to you.
Amen.

Restore

Restore to me the joy of your salvation and grant me
a willing spirit, to sustain me. —Psalm 51:12 NIV

Everyone goes through hard times in life. What seems to be an insurmountable tragedy to one person may be no big deal to another. We have to remember that we cannot judge another person's experience and emotions, even if we have gone through similar situations. Everyone's circumstances, background, resources, support, outlook, and maturity in faith are different.

Your students may do something wrong and think, *What's the big deal?* But your perspective may be that it is a huge infraction of the rules. Someone may have hurt your feelings and think that you're overreacting, but you are crushed by what they said or did. Prayer, communication, humility, time, and forgiveness are the keys to restoration. God will sustain and restore you if you ask.

If you, a friend, or a relationship in your life needs restoring, I pray that you will remember God's love and forgiveness, and begin the restoration process.

Jesus, your salvation is my joy. Restore what has
been broken in my life and in others'. Amen.

Give Thanks to the Lord

Give thanks to the LORD, for he is good.
His love endures forever. —PSALM 136:1 NIV

Do you regularly take time to remember how good God is and has been? Psalm 136 is a recounting by Israel of God's goodness to them, from His being the one true God, to creation, to bringing them out of slavery in Egypt, to being with them in the wilderness, to forgiving them, to giving them the Promised Land, and finally to His daily love and provision. Every sentence of thanks is followed by "His love endures forever." He has been good, He is good, and He always will be good.

As we near Thanksgiving, you may have an upcoming lesson that will involve your students drawing, telling, or writing about what they are thankful for. I want to encourage you to read all of Psalm 136 and then write your own psalm recounting His goodness and mercy in your life—as Creator, Savior, Sustainer, Provider, Teacher, Guide, and so on.

Lord, I look back to see what you have done,
and I give you thanks. I look ahead with faith,
and I give you thanks. Amen.

Mighty in Battle

Who is this King of glory? The LORD, strong and mighty,
the LORD, mighty in battle! –PSALM 24:8 ESV

I was a military brat from the day I was born, and then I became a military wife, so I'm very familiar with the "warfare" that goes on at home while the military member is away serving. We witnessed and experienced the military members deploy out the front door and the spiritual enemy storm in through the back door. The washer would flood the house and the car would break, and our home was even robbed more than once. Fear and worry distract and at times depress. Relationship issues blow up, major decisions need to be made, children get sick or act out and get in trouble, and the list goes on and on. Warfare rages on the frontlines as well as on the home front.

Perhaps you are a military spouse or have military families at your school. Know that the Lord is mighty in your battle too.

Lord, I pray for our military. Enable me to comfort
and serve their families as they serve our country. Amen.

Rethinking Thankfulness

"Therefore I will give thanks to You, O LORD,
among the nations, and I will sing praises to Your name."
−2 SAMUEL 22:50

If only our students would cheer when we handed out tests, saying, "Thank you! Now I can show you how much I've learned." What if they thanked us for homework and the opportunity to practice and master their material?

Let's rethink thankfulness, turning our complaining into thanksgiving. For example, rethink "I am so busy" to: "Thank God I have things to do, transportation to get there, and people who need me." Or rethink "I have to go to work" to: "Thank you that I am able work and have a paycheck to bring home." When we are frustrated with our family, let's consider that millions of people are praying that they will get married or have children.

Did you know that if you have food in a refrigerator, clothes in a closet, a roof over your head, and a bed to sleep in, you are wealthier than 75 percent of the world's population? Give thanks for what you have, and pray for those in need.

> Lord, help me to rethink what
> I have and express thankfulness. Amen.

Unfailing Love

Answer me quickly, LORD; my spirit fails. Do not hide your face from me or I will be like those who go down to the pit.
—PSALM 143:7 NIV

Report card time can be agonizing. Thinking about students and parents seeing an F on a report card makes my stomach churn and my heart sink.

As difficult as failure in classes or life can be, David cries out in today's verse because of something much deeper. He pleads with God because his spirit itself is failing. His life is in turmoil, he is stretched and stressed beyond words, and he knows nothing on earth can comfort him. Only God's love and guidance can help.

God's love is unfailing. He alone has all the interest, effort, and understanding of our life and our situation. Nothing catches Him off guard; He is always prepared and always follows through. He is faithful, unswerving, and perfect. Why would we look to anyone or anything else?

When life's chaos and concerns swirl around you and you feel your spirit fail, always remember you have a God who never does!

Lord, may I never forget your unfailing love.
Amen.

Devoted and Never Divided

Rejoice in our confident hope. Be patient in trouble,
and keep on praying. –ROMANS 12:12 NLT

Your prayer times are strategic summits each day to fight off the enemy's schemes. If you belong to a family, team, club, or church, you know you have to fight for unity.

The best defense is a strong offense. Resolve now to be devoted to one another before conflicts arise. It is imperative that you pray for one another daily. Satan will not stop trying to destroy your unity. You must keep your eyes open and your hearts softened toward one another so nothing comes between you. Set your mind on unity, and begin planning ways you can serve your school and community together. Accomplishing things together will make you stronger. You will need this strength as you laugh, praise, weep, and humble yourselves together throughout this year and hopefully in many more years to come.

Resolve to be in the Lord's army, adding value to your campus and your community while remaining indivisibly devoted to one another in the family of God.

Lord, I pray that your family will be devoted,
and never divided, as brothers and sisters in Christ. Amen.

Worry Free

"So do not worry about tomorrow, for tomorrow will bring
worries of its own. Today's trouble is enough for today."
—MATTHEW 6:34 NRSV

If anyone ever thought that becoming a Christian would take
away all their troubles, they should be introduced to this verse.
Not only are we not protected from troubles invading our lives,
but we are warned that we will have them on a daily basis. So
how do we benefit as Christians?

God never says, "I didn't see that coming." He sees everything coming long before it arrives. How many days (or night's
sleeps) have we wasted by worrying about something that never
came to pass? We miss the opportunities of today because we're
worrying about the what-ifs of tomorrow. Then we put off the
responsibilities of today because we're too tired from worrying
about tomorrow.

What worry is weighing you down today? Stop now and pray
about it. Focus on today and what needs to get done, and don't
delay the blessings of today by worrying about tomorrow.

> Lord, help me to remember that I don't need to worry
> about tomorrow because you're already there. Amen.

Expressing Thankfulness

Let them give thanks to the LORD for his unfailing love and
his wonderful deeds for mankind. –PSALM 107:31 NIV

salm 107 contains forty-three verses that list reasons to be
thankful and how to express thankfulness. Here are a few of
the examples:

- *He guides when we cannot find our way.* Some of us may
  have wandered in the desert of decision, wondering
  what to do with our life, where to live, or who to share
  it with. We are faced with many tough decisions. Give
  thanks that He guides us.
- *He forgives our sins and breaks the chains that hold us in the
  bondage of guilt.* Guilt holds us captive; we suffer mentally, physically, and spiritually. Some people know God
  forgives, but they still hold on to guilt. Receive His forgiveness, and thank Him for taking your sin and guilt.
- *He saves us from distress, affliction, and troubles.* God rescues
  and heals. Thank Him for the times that He has rescued, healed, or restored you.
- *He meets our needs, rewards our faith, and blesses us in ways
  we never imagined.* Thank Him for what He has given to
  you and yours.

Lord, I pray that you would be exalted through
my expressed thankfulness. Amen.

Tuned In

For, "Whoever would love life and see good days must keep
his tongue from evil and his lips from deceitful speech."
—1 PETER 3:10 NIV

In my family, we usually keep our radios tuned to Christian stations; we view it as an opportunity to worship while we drive. One day, after picking my car up from the mechanic, the radio host cussed twice while discussing a current event. I was so confused!

Of course the station had been changed, and it got me thinking about our mouths. Our friends, neighbors, and family who know we're Christians and even the people who see our Christian bumper sticker or have heard us say, "I'll pray for you," have expectations of what they think they should hear coming out of our mouths. If they have the wrong idea about Christians, surprise them with love and kindness.

Inappropriate language or jokes, gossip, judgment, and so on sends the wrong signal and damages our influence in their lives. May we be careful of what we say so they don't "tune us out" when we talk about faith and Scripture. Let your love for Jesus and His goodness fill your mouth and all your conversations.

Lord, keep my lips from evil and
my friends "tuned in." Amen.

Let Grace Set the Pace

> Justified by faith, we have peace with God through our
> Lord Jesus Christ, through whom also we have obtained
> our introduction by faith into this grace in which we stand;
> and we exult in hope of the glory of God. –ROMANS 5:1–2

In difficult times, we tend to either rejoice or retreat. Think about how your students handle difficulties. Of course you see a broad spectrum of responses because your students come from different backgrounds, experiences, resources, intelligence levels, personalities, and so on. But none of those things are the defining factors for gain through pain.

Reread today's Scripture verses. It is when we stand in a state of grace that we exult in both the terrific and turbulent days. We need to understand that our circumstances do not define our character; they can only be used to prove and strengthen it.

In Christ we exult in hope. *Exult* means to revel, rejoice, boast, take pride, and triumph. We get to revel in triumph through the tough times. We get to show the world what it means to walk in faith, stand in grace, and win the race.

Lord, let your grace set the pace
in everything I face. Amen.

The Least of These

"The King will reply, 'I tell you the truth,
whatever you did for one of the least of these brothers
of mine, you did for me.'" –MATTHEW 25:40 NIV

One of my most favorite organizations to work with is Operation Christmas Child. Each year, shoeboxes filled with toys, hygiene items, crayons, hairclips, baseballs, and more are distributed around the world to some of the neediest children on the planet. Each child is also given a book in their own language that explains the gospel, and they are given opportunities to learn about God and the Bible through a continuing program called "The Greatest Journey."

I was blessed in the summer of 2012 to go to Ecuador and help distribute five hundred shoeboxes. Imagine my shock to see children hug toothpaste and cry because Jesus answered their prayer for deodorant. Amazing!

There are lots of wonderful ministries out there to help us give to "the least of these." How can you make a habit of serving those in need? Jesus says that when we serve these, it is actually Him we are serving.

Lord, may I always remember that Jesus said,
"Whatever you did for the least of these brothers of mine,
you did for me." Amen.

Boast in Our King

Now I know that the LORD saves His anointed;
He will answer ... with the saving strength of His
right hand. Some boast in chariots ... but we will boast
in the name of the LORD, our God. –PSALM 20:6–7

Getting to choose our leaders and representatives is one of the greatest aspects of living in America. We have a voice, which is a privilege many countries do not have. Whether we're voting for a president or our school board members, we know we need God-fearing, Jesus-following, Spirit-filled candidates.

The most important decision we will ever make is, "Who will be my King? Who will I live for?" We need to profess our love and trust in Jesus. He has our best interest at heart, and selflessly sacrificed His life for ours. He is our real hope.

If elections have divided your school or district, take some time today to pray and act in ways that will restore unity. Pray for your country, your city, and your district. Intercede for friends, family, or even schools that are divided because of politics instead of united in love and purpose.

> Lord, help us to be united,
> and to boast in you as our King. Amen.

Carefree

Cast your cares on the LORD and he will sustain you;
he will never let the righteous be shaken. –PSALM 55:22 NIV

Truly casting our cares on the Lord is sometimes easier said than done. It takes practice and faith to release the worry and rely on Jesus. Casting our cares means giving up the thought of having control; it reveals our trust in God as a result of knowing Him through His Word and faithfulness. He is sovereign, supreme with all knowledge and power. He is sufficient in ways we could never accomplish or imagine.

Casting our cares enables us to live "carefree," and is not to be confused with being careless or uncaring. Casting our cares on Christ takes great love and strength, as we must release the burden and grab hold of His hand to guide and sustain us through great pain and even great gain. Having a carefree life means giving all our circumstances to Him; it means swapping worry for worship.

> Lord, I cast my cares on you because you care
> for me in ways I cannot even imagine. I am steadfast,
> not shaken, in your hands. Amen.

Tested

Declare me innocent, O Lord, for I have acted
with integrity; I have trusted in the Lord without wavering.
Put me on trial, Lord, and cross-examine me.
Test my motives and my heart. —Psalm 26:1–2 NLT

As educators, we know what a test is. It's a tool that one in
authority uses to upset, stress, sadden, or humiliate another,
right? Of course not! Why, then, do we give tests? To prove that
our students learned what is necessary, and that they are ready to
move on to higher learning.

So why do we get so shaken up when God allows us to be
tested? It's easy to say that God is our Lord, but quite another to
prove that we will obey Him no matter what. Exodus 16:4 shows
us that sometimes we are tested to prove our obedience, and in
the end we get to prove God's faithfulness. 2 Chronicles 32 challenges us. We bless God when He gives, but will we bless Him
when He takes away? A genuine heart passes the test.

> Lord, I pray the test I take will prove me genuine,
> with no retake necessary. Amen.

Overflowing

My cup overflows with blessings.
—PSALM 23:5 NLT

A thankful heart is a happy heart, filled and overflowing with the realization of bountiful blessings that sustain and even spoil us at times. Trials and challenges come and go, but God's blessings are in constant flow—everything from our heart beating, to the love that fills it, to the people and opportunities in our life, to sunsets and so many other blessings overflowing our cup.

Counting and naming our blessings is not only a great stress reducer; it is also commanded by God over and over again. Throughout Scripture, He tells His people to remember and receive His faithful deeds and goodness to build their faith, teach the next generation, and give Him due thanks and glory.

Thanksgiving Day should be a celebration of the culmination of 364 other days of giving thanks for His abundant blessings. Count and name your blessings, write them down, and share God's faithfulness and love with others throughout the year.

Lord, your abundant blessings overflow my life.
May my thanks and praise overflow your throne. Amen.

Speak Truth in Love

> Instead, speaking the truth in love, we will grow
> to become in every respect the mature body of him
> who is the head, that is, Christ. –EPHESIANS 4:15 NIV

I do not recall Jesus tossing the disciples overboard because they were afraid. Christ's approach was compassionate, kind, and gentle. Gentleness is an approach, not a retreat. Our approach should align with Christ's approach to the sinners He encountered in Scripture.

Likewise, we do not attack our students with angry words and criticism when they are failing; we reach out with real concern and try to help them succeed. We work and listen to understand the root of their issue and then help them overcome it. Criticism repels people; love draws them.

People are hurting in ways we don't know or understand; they are seeking love, encouragement, and acceptance from anyone who will give it to them. Gangs and cults prey on outcasts who feel rejected and are willing to do anything to belong. The church needs to be a safe and loving place for the wayward and wounded soul. As the church, how can Christians—and you particularly—do this?

Lord, help me speak the truth in love
with gentleness and compassion and live in a way
that draws others to you. Amen.

The Testimony of Thanks

> Oh give thanks to the LORD … make known His deeds. …
> sing praises to Him; speak of all His wonders. Glory in His
> holy name; let the heart of those who seek the LORD be glad.
> Remember His wonderful deeds which He has done.
>
> —1 CHRONICLES 16:8–10, 12

Giving thanks reminds us of our dependency on God's faithfulness to sustain and even surpass our needs. Practicing giving thanks will form a much-needed prayer habit that will focus us on the blessing instead of the busyness of the season.

Many people are afraid to witness to others. Thanksgiving makes it easy to share Jesus because it gives us a chance to testify about how thankful we are for His wonderful deeds. No one can deny His blessings in our life.

Tell God thank you every time you think of something you are grateful for. If you can, share one testimony of His wonderful deeds in your life, allow time for everyone to share, and make sure you continue or repeat this activity if your school is in session over Thanksgiving week.

Lord, let me celebrate Thanksgiving every day.
Let my life and lips testify of your wonderful deeds. Amen.

More

But as for me, I will hope continually,
and will praise You yet more and more. –PSALM 71:14

Christmastime is drawing closer, and students are busy making out their wish lists. If you could ask for more of something for Christmas, what would it be? More time? More money? More shoes? More sleep?

We could all use *more*–to know God more, to trust Him more, and to spend more time talking with Him. We need to tell more people that He loves them more than they can comprehend. We want to love Him more, to be more obedient. And we want to praise Him more, memorize more Scripture, and give more in ministry.

It delights Jesus to hear us say, "I want to spend more time with you, get to know you more, and hear more of what you want and think." Scripture tells us that that if we seek His kingdom and righteousness first, all that we need will be added to us. He will supply more than we ever dreamed or imagined. Set your heart on more of Him.

> Lord, kindle in me the desire
> to know you more. Amen.

Focus on the Father

Until I come, give attention to the public reading of
Scripture, to exhortation and teaching. –1 TIMOTHY 4:13

God's Word is as relevant today as it was the day it was written; He reveals His story and Himself. We see His heart, His plans, His power, and so much more, on every page and in every chapter.

As you read to see what God is revealing about Himself, ask yourself, "How does God want me to respond to Him?" Keeping the focus on the Father gives us a humble and healthy perspective of His love and awesomeness. This perspective helps us realize the value of our character and choices.

God has plans for every aspect of your life based on His love and your kingdom value. It may be difficult to grasp His love if you did not experience love and acceptance from your earthly father. Take time to pray, asking God to reveal Himself and to prompt you on how you should respond to His revelation in a way that will delight and glorify Him.

> Lord, I desire to focus on you as you reveal
> yourself and your will to me. Amen.

Many Members Yet One Body

For even as the body is one and yet has many members,
and all the members of the body, though they are many,
are one body, so also is Christ. … And if one member
suffers, all the members suffer with it; if one member
is honored, all the members rejoice with it.
—1 CORINTHIANS 12:12, 26

When I started writing devotionals for educators, it was a small ministry. Now God has blessed it, and educators around the world use them to gather together in prayer.

Prayer has always been what holds us together—the greatest resource we all hold in common despite our otherwise massive diversity. Some educators meet in beautiful buildings, while others meet under a tree. Together, we pray for our marriages, families, job security, parents, students, nations, and resources—from computers and crayons to toilet paper and clean drinking water.

Through every trial, always be sure of these two things: First, God loves you and is working on your behalf, and second, an enormous group of educators are holding you up in prayer.

> Lord, thank you for one body in Christ
> that lifts me up in prayer. Amen.

Ponder

Great are the works of the Lord; they are pondered
by all who delight in them. —Psalm 111:2 niv

In this busy world, it seems like a luxury to sit and ponder anything besides what we need to get done. But I encourage you to stop and ponder God's goodness. Pray over anything that pulls your attention away from Him, and treat distractions as a prayer prompt.

This time between the thoughtful season of Thanksgiving and the gift-giving season of Christmas is the perfect time to consider the gifts we have received from God and to give thanks for the everyday blessings He provides.

Ponder a wonderful gift from God that delights your heart, besides the gifts we are all thankful for (our salvation, family, and friends). Focus on and thank God for something that you had not imagined or expected, such as an experience, opportunity, or something achieved or received. What have you done with that gift, and how did it change your life? Did you use it some way for the kingdom? Do you still thank God for it once in a while? If not, do so now. He is a generous God.

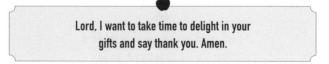

Lord, I want to take time to delight in your
gifts and say thank you. Amen.

Deck Your Heart

"And you, my child, will be called a prophet
of the Most High; for you will go on before the Lord
to prepare the way for him, to give his people
the knowledge of salvation." –LUKE 1:76–77 NIV

Does your December "prepare the way" for the Lord? Our lives can quickly become distracted from the true meaning and attitude of Christmas. Crowded stores and full calendars lead to stress instead of holiday cheer. Decorating and baking and all that we do is enough to make us crazy. But *crazy* is not the spirit of Christmas. It is vital for unbelievers to see the peace that Jesus brought to earth that first Christmas, and they won't see it if Christians don't show it.

Many teachers get out of school only a few days before Christmas, so get started now. Deck your halls early so you can "deck your heart" in December and prepare a clear path for Jesus to saturate your season. It gives you time to help others and to share the joy of Christ's arrival for our salvation. Do whatever you can now so that you can enjoy and rejoice during your Christmas break.

> Lord, may I prepare the way to your
> home and heart. Amen.

December

Blessed to Be a Blessing

As each one has received a special gift, employ it in serving
one another as good stewards of the manifold grace of God.
—1 PETER 4:10

As we enter the gift-giving season, ponder the point that God gives us gifts for the benefit of His church and kingdom. He is telling us that we are blessed to be a blessing. In addition to blessing others, our gifts are also purposed to bring God glory and thanksgiving. We are to recognize Him as the Giver of all gifts, knowing that He will multiply our efforts and the results and enrich us in the process as we minister to others.

What could you do for or give to someone that would multiply ministry and prompt praise? It doesn't necessarily have to cost you money; your time and talent are amazing gifts too. Imagine the impact of giving someone something that might equip them to benefit another life. What would it mean to you to have a Merry Ministering Christmas?

Lord, I commit to act on the knowledge
that I am blessed to be a blessing. Amen.

Consider the Helpless

How blessed is he who considers the helpless,
the LORD will deliver him in a day of trouble. –PSALM 41:1

Reading the psalms of King David can be like riding an emotional roller coaster. In addition to the many victories, David had his share of hurts and helplessness. Scripture tells of his despair as he was pursued by Saul and armies, when he hid in the wilderness and fought battles. Other times he sinned and reaped great punishment. He suffered emotional despair, illness, and heartbreak, from the behavior of his children to the loss of a baby.

Some people at your school are suffering some of these same heartbreaks. Perhaps you have military families who are separated, with spouses and children worried about their loved one serving overseas. Maybe someone has lost or become estranged from a child.

In David's times of helplessness, God sent people to hearten and help restore him, and David responded by writing psalms that serve as a reminder today. God blesses those who are a blessing to others, and He remembers those who remember others. How can you hearten and restore a someone-in-need in your life?

Lord, may I consider the helpless
this holiday season and always. Amen.

Serve One Another

> But through love serve one another.
> —GALATIANS 5:13

Christmas is my favorite holiday and our halls are always decked along with every other room in the house. One Christmas, I was sick and weak from my chemo treatments and had concluded that we would have to keep our decorating simple at best. My creative-thinking friends, busy teachers no less, knew that I had tried so hard to keep life as normal as possible for my family during my illness, and they thought Christmas should be no exception. Although they had a long list of things they needed to do to prepare, there was joy and laughter as we decorated my house together. My family would have celebrated without decorations. But we were blessed with a beautiful home, and it wasn't one more thing my young children would miss because I was sick. It may seem trivial, even petty, but it meant the world to us.

Why am I talking about this in early fall? Christmas can be a difficult time for many people at your school. I encourage you to ask nearby churches to help buy presents and food for families in need. Pull a team together and spread the real Christmas spirit.

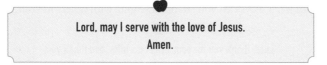

Lord, may I serve with the love of Jesus.
Amen.

Not Lacking Any Gift

December is referred to as the gift-giving season. With so many celebrations, it's probable that many students are gearing up to write out their wish list.

Have you started your gift list? In preparing for the spirit of the season, read the Scriptures below, noting the italicized gifts we have been given. Ponder these gifts during this season to keep a perspective on the Gift that is the real reason we celebrate during this time of year.

- Romans 3:24: "*Being justified* as a gift by His grace through the redemption which is in Christ Jesus."
- Romans 6:23: "For the wages of sin is death, but the free gift of God is *eternal life* in Christ Jesus our Lord."
- Ephesians 2:8: "For by *grace* you have been *saved* through faith; and that not of yourselves, it is the gift of God."
- Psalm 84:11: "For the LORD God is a *sun and shield*; the LORD gives *grace and glory*; no good thing does He withhold from those who walk uprightly."
- Romans 15:5: "Now may the God who gives *perseverance and encouragement* grant you to be of the same mind with one another according to Christ Jesus."

In what ways can you share these gifts with others in your life?

Lord, thank you for your priceless gifts, and thank you for sending your Son, Jesus, the greatest Gift of all. Amen.

Full of Love

"I am the LORD, the LORD. I am a God who is tender
and kind. I am gracious. I am slow to get angry.
I am faithful and full of love." –EXODUS 34:6 NIRV

Mr. Jones sat in angst on the first day of school. He hated children and couldn't stand their chattering voices, especially if they were talking to him. He constantly thought of ways to make them miserable and planned the hardest lessons to exasperate them into failure. He refused their pleas for help, saying, "You should have read your book and paid attention to my lecture."

Hopefully you are thinking, *There is no way this Mr. Jones guy teaches*. The point of this crazy made-up example is that, sadly, some people view God this way. They believe He sits up in heaven, thinking of ways to make them fail or be miserable and ignoring their cries for help, saying, "You should have read My Book and listened to those sermons."

God is love! He is not bothered by the sound of your voice but rather delights in your prayers. He is full of love for you.

Lord, you are faithful and full of love.
Amen.

Keep Your Eyes on Jesus

But seeing the wind he became frightened, and beginning
to sink, he cried out, "Lord, save me!" –MATTHEW 14:30

As the date for the school musical drew near, it seemed to the
untrained eye that the choir would not be ready in time; but
to our director, all was on track. She was strongly encouraged
to change the date, but she refused because she knew the plan.
The date was set so that the choir would know the words, their
parts, and the songs well enough to get through the play as long
as they kept their eyes on her. More practice might make them
too self-confident, and then they wouldn't watch her for direction
on the night of the play.

God has set the dates for every opportunity to serve Him
throughout our life. He has prepared us along the way, and when
it comes time to "perform," we may think we're not ready, that
we need more time and training. But He has equipped us to do
the job as long as we keep our eyes on our heavenly Conductor.

Lord, may I trust that you are conducting my life.
Amen.

Christ's Government

> Of the increase of his government and of peace there will be no end, on the throne of David and over his kingdom, to establish it and to uphold it with justice and with righteousness from this time forth and forevermore. The zeal of the LORD of hosts will do this. –ISAIAH 9:7 ESV

We have suffered some difficult years in our nation and around the world. Righteousness and justice are cast aside as we run up more debt, pass more laws that disobey God and persecute Christians, and more. This is not a political statement; it is simply today's news. So how do we remain calm in chaos?

We are citizens of the kingdom of heaven, and Christ's government reigns with peace, justice, and righteousness. Like a child anticipating the gifts of Christmas morning, we can rest assured that all of these will be accomplished for us in perfect measure and will stand forever.

Consider how these times of global stress and national division are affecting your students and school. Despite feeling the pain and strain of these, how is your reaction and resolve different from that of non-believers?

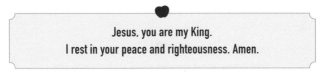

Jesus, you are my King.
I rest in your peace and righteousness. Amen.

Life-Giving Answers Late at Night

> Now there was a man of the Pharisees, named Nicodemus,
> a ruler of the Jews; this man came to Jesus by night and
> said to Him … "How can a man be born when he is old?"
> –JOHN 3: 1–2, 4

Nicodemus was a Pharisee whose heart was changed by his time with Jesus. Read all of John 3 and notice how many questions Nicodemus asked Jesus. It makes me think of the students who hang around after the bell rings because they don't want to ask questions in front of other students, and the more we teach, the more questions they ask. Nicodemus continually asked the clarifying question, "How?"

After Jesus' crucifixion, Nicodemus helped take His body from the cross and prepare it for burial. I wonder if he remembered Jesus telling him, "For God so loved the world, that He gave His only begotten Son" (John 3:16)? Perhaps Nicodemus was even watching for a miracle. And maybe as Jesus gave him answers, Nicodemus found more than solutions; maybe he found a Savior.

Keep this in mind the next time you have a student who seems to ask never-ending questions. Christ never lost patience with those who searched Him out, and with His help, you can do the same.

> Lord, never let me grow weary of students who ask
> many questions nor be too busy to expand on a lesson. Amen.

Foundations of Learning

Doing wickedness is like sport to a fool, and so is wisdom to a man of understanding. What the wicked fears will come upon him, but the desire of the righteous will be granted.
—Proverbs 10:23–24

I once read an article that concluded that early learning in math is key to success in math later. The study concluded that without a good foundation, a student won't do well. I would be so bold as to add that good foundational learning in any subject will increase success as students progress—and that this is also true in life.

Life builds on itself. Opportunities to see God move and using that knowledge in other experiences increases our faith and success. We are empowered, educated, and enlightened by His Spirit in us. We can usually look back at past experiences, both trials and victories, and learn from them.

Apply what you have learned earlier to current situations, even if the situation or equation is different. Foundational facts will still help you come to a successful resolution.

Lord, help me to use a firm faith foundation of early learning that increases my success and progress. Amen.

Now Listen

Then the angel told her: Do not be afraid, Mary,
for you have found favor with God. Now listen:
You will conceive and give birth to a son,
and you will call His name Jesus. –LUKE 1:30–33 HCSB

Just imagine having an angel stand before you and tell you that you have found favor with God. Imagine being told not to be afraid, when your heart is racing and your knees are knocking. Imagine that you have been given news that will not only change your world but the whole world.

Except for the angel's appearance, you don't have to imagine this; it is a part of every believer's life. We have found favor with God, so much so that He sent His one and only Son.

We have been told not to be afraid. Deuteronomy 31:6 says, "Be strong and courageous, do not be afraid or tremble at them, for the LORD your God is the one who goes with you. He will not fail you or forsake you."

We have been told the good news that has forever changed our life, and we can change the lives of everyone we share it with, for eternity.

> Lord, I have listened. Help me to share the good news
> of Christ's birth this holiday season. Amen.

The Glory in Authority

Because of the privilege and authority God has given me,
I give each of you this warning: Don't think you are better
than you really are. –ROMANS 12:3 NLT

It's amazing to watch and work with people who serve through God's authority. Participating in life-changing challenges, when you know it is for God's glory and the greater-good of the students and your school, is a delight. It's refreshing to see others putting their careers on the line for the sake of the students or calling out unethical behavior or decisions. Perhaps one of the greatest gifts is to work with leaders who pray and obey.

You may be thinking about a negative situation concerning a political or abusive staff member. It may seem like they have the upper hand for now, but God will not allow them to prevail. Keep praying, "Your kingdom come, your will be done, in my classroom, in our school, and in our district and state as it is in heaven." Your prayers and position under God's authority bring light to dark places and agendas.

Lord, I know all authority is for your glory.
Amen.

Love

> Love is patient, love is kind and is not jealous;
> love does not brag and is not arrogant, does not act
> unbecomingly; it does not seek its own, is not provoked,
> does not take into account a wrong suffered, does not
> rejoice in unrighteousness, but rejoices with the truth;
> bears all things, believes all things, hopes all things,
> endures all things. Love never fails. —1 CORINTHIANS 13:4–8

Would you agree that we overuse the word *love*? Saying "I love
…" tends to lead to a list of our favorite things. To combat
this, try to use other words in place of *love* when the word really
doesn't apply to the degree of your affection. More importantly,
focus on expressing love the way God instructs.

Agape love is unconditional; it is the love of today's verses.
God calls us to a love that sacrifices, that gives with no expectation of receiving; it thinks of the other person above self. God
calls us to love in a way that is respectful and doesn't say or do
things that disrespect God or the other person.

> Lord, may I know and show the love you
> desire for us to receive and give. Amen.

Free Gift

For the wages of sin is death, but the free gift of God
is eternal life in Christ Jesus our Lord. –ROMANS 6:23

Christmas shopping can be tons of fun or make us feel like we've been hit by a ton of bricks. We search for the perfect gift, wondering if we should buy something people want or something they need. Questions abound: Will it last or break before Christmas dinner? Will it get used or tossed in a closet? Can we afford it? Is it worth it? Will it hold its value over time?

God gave the one true perfect Christmas gift that encompasses all that we want and need. His gift was something we needed more than anything else and more valuable than we could ever afford. *The* Christmas gift is a free gift—the gift of eternal life given to us by Jesus. It is for anyone and everyone; all we have to do is ask. Share this gift with all your friends.

> Lord, may I share Jesus and His free gift of eternal life
> with everyone I know this Christmas season. Amen.

Put It into Practice

He replied, "My mother and brothers are those who
hear God's word and put it into practice." –LUKE 8:21 NIV

No matter what subject we're teaching, the first thing the students need to know is the lingo. The words we use in our lessons are the foundation for everything we teach.

The same is true spiritually. We must know the Word–Jesus–who became flesh and dwelt among us. Without Jesus, we fail the entire subject of life. Our soul starves within us, crying out to be fed, but no matter what we do or what we obtain, it is never satisfied. We must also know the Word of God–the Bible. We must read, study, think, and pray over it and through it daily. Without the Bible, we lack direction for life.

As Christian educators, our role is to help prepare our students for the life God has prepared for them. Our students will see the Word, hear the Word, and learn the Word if we live the Word, putting it into practice every day.

Lord, may I always put your Word into practice.
Amen.

A Child Is Born, a Son Is Given

For to us a child is born, to us a son is given; and the government shall be upon his shoulder, and his name shall be called Wonderful Counselor, Mighty God, Everlasting Father, Prince of Peace. —ISAIAH 9:6 ESV

To us a child is born, the Divine in human flesh, our *only hope* lying in a manger. He was given to us by God, for He so loved the world that He *gave* His one and only Son. These two events, God sending and Jesus coming, are enough to take our breath away. We will never comprehend this miracle fully until we see heaven. Jesus is an everlasting gift; we can never use Him up, and His warrantee doesn't run out. He is truly the Gift that keeps on giving.

As Christmas approaches and your students, coworkers, and their families are making out their Christmas wish lists, pray that they receive the one Gift they truly need, Jesus. During this gift-giving season, give the gift of prayer and share Christ's love and message.

Jesus, you were the Child born, the Son given, our Wonderful Counselor and Prince of Peace. Amen.

The Joy of Your Presence

For you make him most blessed forever; you make him
glad with the joy of your presence. –Psalm 21:6 esv

While sitting in church, I watched a girl dance her way up the
aisle. She skipped and twirled with this beautiful smile on her
face as her father followed close enough to enjoy her dance and
guide her to where they needed to go. Every few rows, she waved
to someone or danced to make them smile.

One man was distracted or had had an exceptionally hard
day, because he didn't smile back or wave when she reached
him. The procession stopped; she waved and danced, but still
no smile. She wrinkled her brow in confusion as her father tried
to scoot her up the aisle. A few moments later, she ran around
her father back to the man and hugged him. He laughed until he
cried, and that man smiled all the way through the service, long
after she danced away.

Are you a joyful person? Is your classroom a joyful place? If
so, where does that joy come from? And if not, what can you do
to bring joy into your life?

Lord, may I know and share the joy
of your presence in your life. Amen.

Complete Joy

I have told you this so that my joy may be in you
and that your joy may be complete. –JOHN 15:11 NIV

Yesterday I shared about the girl determined to share her joy. She wanted to share her joy with everyone, even one who did not initially want it.

We should walk with that joy, staying close enough to our heavenly Father that He enjoys us and can guide us. There are many days when we have copies to make, meetings to attend, and parents to call, and in the midst of it all we forget to bring our joy with us. Be aware of the expression on your face as you walk the halls.

It is easy to share our smile, cooperation, resources, and compassion with those who are easy to get along with, but what about the one who is never happy? Are we to share our joy in the Lord with everyone, even the extra-effort people? Can we really throw our hands up and walk away, muttering, "They will never change"? Of course not. God never gave up on us.

Lord, may I experience and share joy, in all and with all.
Joy to the world, the Lord is come!

With All Your Heart

"For I know the plans that I have for you," declares
the LORD, "plans for welfare and not for calamity to give
you a future and a hope. Then you will call upon Me and
come and pray to Me, and I will listen to you. You will
seek Me and find Me when you search for Me with
all your heart." –JEREMIAH 29:11–13

Many people quote Jeremiah 29:11 as their life verse, yet it was
originally written to Jews who were exiled in Babylon. It was
God's promise to turn their circumstances for good when they
sought Him with their whole heart.

The good news is that Christians today can also claim this
verse. Just like the Jews did, we face consequences for our sin.
And also just like for the Jews, today's Scripture reminds us that
God is bigger than any sin we commit.

God had a plan for your life before you were even conceived,
and it is a plan for welfare and hope. Sin leads us away from this
good path, but we can always find it again when we seek God
with all our heart.

Lord, may I seek you every day with
all my heart. Amen.

Preparing for Christmas

> They went on their way, and the star they had seen
> when it rose went ahead of them until it stopped over
> the place where the child was. When they saw the star,
> they were overjoyed. —MATTHEW 2:9–10 NIV

Christmastime seems to come to our department stores earlier every year. I have even seen Christmas decorations for sale in July. I had to laugh, knowing there are other people like me out there who prepare for Christmas all year long.

As educators, preparation for Christmastime is paramount. Every December, I receive prayer requests about chaos, legal defense for expressions of faith, and exhaustion. It breaks my heart how we battle through a season whose message is "peace on earth."

The wise men help us remember the value of preparing for Christmas. They probably learned from Daniel's prophecies to watch for a great king, and they did watch, waiting eagerly, fully prepared for that first Christmas to arrive.

Prepare for Christmas now, personally and legally, so you are ready to worship and enjoy the season and the Savior.

Lord, help me prepare to come and worship you.
Amen.

Childlike

And He said: "I tell you the truth, unless you
change and become like children, you will never enter
the kingdom of heaven." —MATTHEW 18:3 NIV

One Sunday I saw a teenage girl looking around uncomfortably outside our church, wearing clothes that did not seem quite appropriate. I asked if I could help her find someone. She said her friend had invited her to church, but she probably wasn't expecting her since she had asked her every week for months.

People stared and threw looks of disapproval at her as we walked down the aisle to the front pews where our youth sit. I saw her friend jump up and climb over people to throw her arms around her neck. Some of the other youth were saying, "Yay, you came!" and "Wow, come sit by us." The girl was smiled at and hugged as she made her way down the row to sit in the middle of the group. Two months later, she was baptized. The youth stood and cheered as if they were at a football game. Thank God for her friend's invitation and her acceptance.

Lord, make me more childlike in love.
Amen.

Known by Name

"You have said, 'I know you by name and you
have found favor with me.'" –Exodus 33:12 NIV

In this verse, God has told Moses, "I know you by name and
you have found favor with me." God knows you by name too,
and He loves you very much. He also knows each of your family
members, friends, coworkers, students, and neighbors by name.
He knows everything about you and everything about them.
They have been placed within your reach and influence so you
can share the love and message of Jesus with one another.

Pray as you walk around your school. Pray throughout the
day when you pass by someone or find out a need they have.
Pray through your neighborhood, as you drive to and from
school every day. Learn student's names who are not in your
class and listen for conversations in the halls that prompt you
to pray. Pray in doorways for every person who passes through,
and ponder what God might have planned for the people in your
reach and how you can serve Him by helping them.

> Lord, may I find strength in being known by you
> and serving others to make you known. Amen.

Limited Time Only

Why, you do not even know what will happen tomorrow.
What is your life? You are a mist that appears for a little
while and then vanishes. –JAMES 4:14 NIV

Advertisers often warn, "Limited time only," to get our attention and urge us to act quickly so we don't miss out. Imagine the thought process that led to this devotion when my son pulled the "limited time only" sticker off the new chip bag from our pantry and stuck it on his forehead.

We have hundreds of "limited time only" experiences in and out of the classroom. What do you do with that limited time? In the classroom, what do you want your students to learn from you? And out of the classroom, is God prompting you to do something that you have hesitated to do?

Think about what you want to be remembered for. We live a "limited time only" life. Have you been hesitant to give encouragement to someone or plant some seeds of God's love? Today, imagine your class with "limited time only" stickers on their foreheads.

> Lord, may I not hesitate to share
> what you have placed on my heart. Amen.

Study the Great Works of the Lord

Praise the LORD! I will give thanks to the LORD with all my heart, in the company of the upright and in the assembly.
—PSALM 111:1

There are many busy and tiring seasons for educators. Amid these, the best prescription for tiredness is giving thanks, and perseverance is strengthened with praise.

God calls us to remember His wonders, works, and wisdom that have guided, protected, and blessed us throughout our lives. We have an obligation to share His splendid and majestic works as a testimony of our relationship with Him as almighty God. Our public profession of His Lordship in our lives causes the lost to lean in and take a closer look at the One who is worthy of all obedience and trust.

Our thanks is our testimony of His ongoing love and hand in our lives, the reason for our steadfastness in times of trouble, the evidence for our faith instead of fear, and a reminder to us that He has made Himself known in our lives.

Lord, may I really study the great works you have done in my life so I give you the thanks you deserve. Amen.

Joy

For You, O LORD, have made me glad by what
You have done, I will sing for joy at the works
of Your hands. –PSALM 92:4

"Joy to the world! The Lord has come; let earth receive her
King; let every heart prepare Him room, and heaven and na-
ture sing." Isaac Watt's carol "Joy to the World" celebrates the
Savior's mission beyond a season, and few know the third verse:
"No more let sins and sorrows grow, nor thorns infest the ground;
He comes to make His blessings flow far as the curse is found."

The Lord came, He reigns, His blessings flow, and He rules
with truth and grace. Our response is to prepare our hearts, sing
praise, reject the curse of sin, soak in truth, and wonder at His
love. Joy springs from our lives when we prepare room in our
hearts and lives for the Spirit to rule.

As educators, we spend a tremendous amount of time making
other families' Christmases special. God sees your heart and will
fill it with immeasurable joy. Sing! Shout! Share!

> Lord, may joy have its rightful place
> on my face and throughout my days. Amen.

Christmas Story

When the angels went away from them into heaven,
the shepherds said to one another, "Let us go over to
Bethlehem and see this thing that has happened, which the
Lord has made known to us." And they went with haste and
found Mary and Joseph, and the baby lying in a manger.
And when they saw it, they made known the saying that
had been told them concerning this child. And all who
heard it wondered at what the shepherds told them.
But Mary treasured up all these things, pondering them in
her heart. And the shepherds returned, glorifying
and praising God for all they had heard and seen,
as it had been told them. –LUKE 2:15–20 ESV

Take some time to sit and read the Christmas story in Luke 2:1–20. Treasure these words and how they changed your life. If you would like, ponder your favorite Christmas memory or what you love best about this time of the year. Choose to enjoy this moment of peace and prayer. Guard your heart, and do not let anything steal your joy during this season. Wonder at Jesus and His love.

Jesus, I want to make your story known.
Amen.

Renewed and Restored

But they who wait for the LORD shall renew
their strength; they shall mount up with wings like eagles;
they shall run and not be weary; they shall walk
and not faint. —ISAIAH 40:31 ESV

Being an educator can zap our strength physically, mentally, and emotionally, but God says our strength is renewed when we wait on Him. The battle is fought and our fortitude restored when our hope is in God; work, watch, and wait on His hands and plans to bring the challenge to a victory.

We are all works in progress, and sometimes the younger teach the older. Watch children play, sleep, and embrace adventure and new experiences. Take some time this Christmas break and allow yourself to have fun and laugh without thinking about work or worries. Pray and hope in the Lord, then do what He prompts and trust Him for the final results. Wait on Him; He is waiting even now to renew and restore you.

> Lord, you are my hope. I wait on your hand and plan
> to play out as I do my best and trust you for the rest. Amen.

See and Rejoice

When they saw the star, they rejoiced exceedingly
with great joy. —LUKE 2:10 ESV

Have you ever realized that Jesus was willing to come and save us before man was ever created? He truly loved us first! As God spoke and placed the stars in the heavens, He determined the date for Jesus' arrival and set the stars in motion to be in position to guide the wise men to Bethlehem. And when the wise men saw the star, they grabbed their gifts and went to find Him, but their worship began when they saw the star. They "rejoiced exceedingly," so worship was a part of the journey along the way.

Where do we worship Him? Everywhere. Worship is not an hour or so on Sunday; it is an "every day, along the way" lifestyle. "Along the way" to school, running errands, activities, and heading home, we can worship in prayer, music, and sharing the love and message of Jesus—everywhere we go.

> Lord, may the stars remind me every day of Jesus' love,
> and may I respond with great joy. Amen.

Come to Worship

Magi from the east came to Jerusalem and asked,
"Where is the one who has been born king of the Jews?
We saw his star when it rose and have come to worship him."
—MATTHEW 2:1–2 NIV

When my niece was born, we traveled to Georgia from my parents' house in Florida (thankfully by car and not by camel), packed with presents. We were so excited, chatting about who she might look like, what personality she might have, and how she was going to drastically change the lives of my brother and sister-in-law. We discussed how first-time parents don't realize how a child will consume their hearts, and how when the baby comes, love floods their lives.

I wonder what the Magi talked about on their long journey. Did they wonder what this King and His family would look like? Or perhaps they considered what His personality would be and how He would rule the Jews. Did they have any idea how Christ would change our lives, consuming us with love we never imagined? Ponder what you think they talked about on their way home after the dream and seeing the King.

Jesus, I want to take this time to seek
and worship you, our King. Amen.

Opened Hearts, Opened Treasures

On coming to the house, they saw the child with his mother Mary, and they bowed down and worshiped him. Then they opened their treasures and presented him with gifts of gold, frankincense, and myrrh. –MATTHEW 2:11 NIV

The Magi came to the house and found Jesus with His mother and bowed down to worship Him immediately. Here we learn to worship with our hearts first, then with our service and gifts. They offered Him gold, as to a king; frankincense, as to God, for they honored God with the smoke of incense; and myrrh, first as a priest, because it was the first ingredient in the holy anointing oil made by Moses, and second as a man who would suffer and die, for myrrh was also used in embalming dead bodies.

The Messiah had come, given as the greatest gift that mankind could ever receive. God gave first, and anything we have to offer Him we obtained through His gifts and blessings. Whatever we give to God, we first give our hearts and then we give our treasures.

Lord, may I open my heart and my treasures
to present to Jesus. Amen.

After Jesus Was Born...

> When [the Magi] saw the star, they rejoiced. ... After coming into the house they saw the Child with Mary His mother; and they fell to the ground and worshiped Him. Then, opening their treasures, they presented to Him gifts of gold, frankincense, and myrrh. —MATTHEW 2:10–11

I am thankful that the Gospels take us all the way through Jesus' life. Jesus' genealogy, humble birth, life and lessons, cross and empty tomb, and ascension all teach and touch us. The Gospels are filled with Jesus' words, wonder, lessons, commands, conversations, miracles, promises, examples, and, most of all, love. He showed us how to live out His love and how simple it is to share His message.

If you've never read through the Gospels, let me encourage you to do so. Reading them is a great way to start everyday Bible reading. More importantly, it is the best way to saturate ourselves with the supremacy of Jesus. Wise men (and women) still seek Him as we live out HIStory!

> Jesus, like those who followed the star,
> I follow your Word to adore and worship you. Amen.

Praiseworthy

Finally, brothers, whatever is true, whatever is honorable,
whatever is just, whatever is pure, whatever is lovely,
whatever is commendable, if there is any excellence, if there
is anything worthy of praise, think about these things. –
PHILIPPIANS 4:8 ESV

What makes somebody worthy of praise? Think about how you feel when students come back to praise you for the positive contribution you were/are in their lives. Your actions flow from your character, and your character flows from what is in your heart and mind. Philippians 4:9 takes it a step further and says to put them into practice; we tend to do the things we think about.

Today's verse reminds us of what we should keep in mind. We need to direct our thoughts, taking each one captive and holding it to these standards. The brain can be a battlefield of things that are less than pure or not even true. Our thoughts can wander off toward worry or, worse case, stumble into sin and angle off into anger or angst. We have to set our mind on these things and stay the course.

> Lord, I desire for my mind and character to remain
> steadfast in these thoughts and practices. Amen.

January

New View

Therefore, if anyone is in Christ, the new creation has come:
The old has gone, the new is here! —2 Corinthians 5:17 niv

New Year's Day often begins a time of renewed hope and re-solve to improve our lives. I don't find it coincidental that this hope at New Year's follows so closely after our celebration of Christ's birth. But the newness Jesus offers is not like the new-ness of a new year, during which our resolve so often fails us and we soon fall short of our goals. As one salesman told my family when we joined his gym, "We fill up in the beginning of January, but don't worry. It'll clear out in a couple weeks."

Far from this fickle resolution, the newness Jesus brings is rooted in His faithfulness and the promise that what He did for us on the cross is complete. Because of what He has done for us, we can wake up every morning and cheer, "Happy New Life!" Then we can carry our new life with us to our students and inspire them with hope of newness that lasts.

Lord, I praise you for newness that lasts
through all my days. Amen.

Laws of Motion

So be careful to do what the LORD your God has
commanded you; do not turn aside to the right or to
the left. Walk in obedience to all that the LORD your God
has commanded you, so that you may live and prosper
and prolong your days in the land that you will possess.

—DEUTERONOMY 5:32–33 NIV

Newton's Law of Motion states that an object will not move, stop, or change its path of movement unless acted upon by a force. This law also applies to us spiritually, as our human behavior starts, stops, and is steered through the work of the Holy Spirit. He not only directs us but also *causes* fruit in our lives. We are moved by His might as we allow Him to be the Lord of our life.

As educators, we get two New Year's Days—the first day of the new school year and January first. Pray as you move into the new year, asking God to be the force to move, change, or stop you. Allow Him to compel you in the way you should go and the things you should do.

Holy Spirit, set my life in motion.
Amen.

Steadfast Spirit

Create in me a clean heart, O God, and renew
a steadfast spirit within me. –Psalm 51:10

It takes prayer and patience to get back on track after the Christmas holidays, so make a point to emphasize the newness of the year and the opportunities ahead. Your faithful living will result in changing your life, your school, and your community from average to awesome, making a more faith-filled nation and a fuller kingdom.

Pray *big*. You cannot ask for anything too big or too hard for God. Ask God every morning, "What is your purpose for me today, Lord?" Then watch expectantly and excitedly for what He will do in you and through you.

With this start of the new year, ask your students to write down their goals for the year, and then ask frequently how they are holding up. Think of ways you can encourage them to resolve to fight the good fight, and ask God to show them His priorities for their lives. As their teacher, give them a few minutes a couple of times a week to journal and talk about this journey. Just imagine the impact of your commitment and a composition book.

> Lord, I will grasp and pass along a strong
> and steadfast spirit. Amen.

Straight Ahead

Only be strong and very courageous; be careful to do according to the law. ... Do not turn from it to the right or to the left, so that you may have success wherever you go.
–Joshua 1:7

There are a couple of things you can do to start the year worshipping and working straight ahead. One is to ask Jesus to give you a word for the year. Another is to set prayer-supported, godly goals that pertain to your relationships as well as your personal, spiritual, and professional life.

Goals help us focus on God's purpose for our lives so we are not pulled to the left or right by life's distractions. Goals help us prioritize the responsibilities, opportunities, and activities that come our way so that our energy is not depleted before our to-do list. The chance of accomplishing these goals is significantly higher if we write them down and put them somewhere so we see them often.

The world is beckoning for your time. God has many wonderful plans for you this year.

> Lord, may I know and follow your goals, walking straight ahead, and have success wherever I go. Amen.

Don't Concede, Get What You Need

Let us then approach the throne of grace with confidence,
so that we may receive mercy and find grace to help us
in our time of need. —HEBREWS 4:16 NIV

Many New Year's resolutions revolve around a desire to be healthier, thinner, richer, or better educated, or to try something new or improve relationships. I want to ask you to go deeper and ask God to show you where He wants to help you to conform more to the image of Christ.

God enables us every day to be all that He created us to be; we just have to be willing and ask for help. He will work miracles in us if we ask Him to glorify Himself in our needs. Give Him access to every area of your life, and He will supply all that you need.

Lord, thank you that your mercy and strength are
new every morning and that every day can be better,
with new opportunities, new focus, new forgiveness,
and supernatural mercy and grace. Amen.

Prayer Prompts

May the nations be glad and sing for joy, for you rule
the peoples with equity and guide the nations of the earth.
—PSALM 67:4 NIV

I often hear people say, "I want to pray for America, but how many times can you say, 'God bless America'?" People want to know how they can be prompted to spend significant time praying for our nation.

Hundreds of books have probably been written on this subject, but here are my three favorite responses. First, listen to your family and friends. Listen to what they are talking about and worried about—what is happening at school, church, work, and in their families. Listen and pray.

Second, use the "Seven Mountains of Influence" approach and pray for: 1. Education, 2. Family, 3. Church, 4. Government, 5. Business, 6. Military, and 7. Arts, Entertainment & Media. More information on this can be found at http://www.7cultural mountains.org/.

Third, watch and pray through the news stories that catch your heart and attention. As educators, we can also keep a list of things that happen at school each day, students who catch our attention, and situations that frustrate or delight us. Persevere in prayer for each prompt, and thank God for answered prayers.

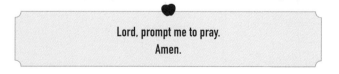

Lord, prompt me to pray.
Amen.

Pause to Ponder the Passages

Your word is a lamp to my feet and a light to my path.
—PSALM 119:105

Jesus, the Word made flesh, poured Himself onto the pages of Scripture long before He poured Himself out on the cross. One of the most powerful ways to pray is to speak God's Word back to Him; it professes faith and proclaims His promises. Let the following verses remind you of the importance of His Word in your life.

- Hebrews 11:3: "By faith we understand that the worlds were prepared by the word of God, so that what is seen was not made out of things which are visible."
- Acts 20:32: "And now I commend you to God and to the word of His grace, which is able to build you up and to give you the inheritance among all those who are sanctified."
- Hebrews 4:12: "For the word of God is living and active and sharper than any two-edged sword, and piercing as far as the division of soul and spirit, of both joints and marrow, and able to judge the thoughts and intentions of the heart."

Personalize each verse with your name and circumstances in your prayers. Practice meditating on His Word by picking a verse and reciting it throughout the day. Write it down and put it somewhere you will see it frequently so it will light your path.

> Lord, your Word lights my path and my prayers.
> Amen.

Keep Your Eyes on the Road

The highway of the upright is to depart from evil;
he who watches his way preserves his life. –Proverbs 16:17

A large protruding barrier interfered with the flow of traffic on a busy road, but the workers were way off the road in a nearby ditch. I later learned that several vehicles had run into that barrier, which spared the lives of the workers. It seems that we are curious beings; our eyes lead and our bodies—or cars—follow.

The same is true of temptation in our lives. Our eyes will pull us off the "highway of the upright," to places of danger and destruction. Think about what turns your head and the heads of your students. Is it something on the Internet, or a video game or TV show? How many times a day do you tell your students, "Watch where you're going"? And what about yourself? Have your eyes strayed, or have you ignored the barriers God has used to warn you? Watch your way, and you will preserve your life.

Lord, may I always keep my eyes on you.
Amen.

His Precepts' Benefits

Bless the LORD, O my soul ... bless His holy name. ...
And forget none of His benefits; who pardons all
your iniquities, who heals all your diseases; who satisfies
your years with good things, so that your youth is
renewed like the eagle. The LORD performs righteous deeds.
—PSALM 103:1–6

In the verses above, the psalmist blesses God for His precepts and passionately commits to continued obedience. Now think of a time when you found yourself a little less passionate about God's rules than the psalmist was. Satan wants us to believe God is depriving us when He expresses His authority, but God's rules are tools for our prosperity blessing and benefit.

As an educator, how do you feel when your instructions are followed? Do you feel respected? Time, effort, and focus are still mandatory, but following the instructions makes the job as painless as possible and ensures that it's accomplished as you required.

Has satan told you that there is gain in pride and rebellion? In disobedience there is always loss. God's statues, precepts, and Word were given for our benefit. Rebellion rejects blessings, while obedience opens heaven's floodgates.

Jesus, I know your precepts are for my benefit.
Amen.

Give Careful Thought to Your Ways

The LORD Almighty says:
"Give careful thought to your ways." –HAGGAI 1:5 NIV

Have you ever told your students to put on their thinking caps? What did you mean by that? Perhaps you were asking a particularly hard question that required a little more concentration. What are some other instances that call for us to adorn our thinking caps?

In previous centuries, judges put on a cap before sentencing criminals. Because judges were respected thinkers, it was referred to as a "thinking cap." Perhaps the criminals should have used their thinking cap earlier to avoid standing before the judge.

God says, "Give careful thought to your ways." Maybe you're thinking through some hard decisions right now. Are you trying or learning something new that requires some extra brain power? Or are you facing a challenge that has been keeping you awake at night? Our thinking caps are an essential part of our everyday wardrobe, but good decisions require more than just thinking it over; we need to pray it over.

Think on God's Word before you decide. The steps are simple: Pray, think, listen, act.

> Jesus, please guide my thoughts
> and decisions so I walk in your way. Amen.

Tricked or Truth

Now there is in Jerusalem by the Sheep Gate a pool,
in Aramaic called Bethesda, which has five roofed
colonnades. In these lay a multitude of invalids—blind,
lame, and paralyzed. One man was there who had been
an invalid for thirty-eight years. –JOHN 5:2–5 ESV

This Bible story is the only described healing at this pool by the Sheep Gate. While in the Holy Land, I visited the pool around one o'clock in the afternoon, as the wind began to stir, which my guide explained was common at that time of day because of a weather/climate phenomenon. John 5:4 mentions angels coming to stir the waters, but this verse has been removed from most Bible versions after it was discovered to be a superstition added to some text many years later as a Greek myth.

Many people, especially the young generation we are teaching, turn to superstition, believing Internet stories and infomercials. Perhaps you have students who challenge your instruction with what they read online. When this happens, pray for God's wisdom so you can help them to separate fact from fiction.

Lord, my days and praise are founded
and fed by your truth. Amen.

Prepared to Persuade, Part 1

Now He who prepared us for this very purpose is God,
who gave to us the Spirit as a pledge. … For we walk by
faith, not by sight. … Therefore we also have
as our ambition, whether at home or absent,
to be pleasing to Him. –2 Corinthians 5:5, 7, 9

As Christians, we have God's Spirit within us. That means we have all the preparation, strength, wisdom, power, patience, joy, courage, faith, and energy we will need if we abide in Him.

Many changes have probably taken place at your school over the years, but today's Scripture tells us to always be of good courage, to walk by faith, and to be ambitious to please God.

Prepare means to perform, accomplish, or achieve.

Ambition is activated or set in motion by love and honor.

Persuade means to induce belief or faith through one's words or behavior.

Understand that God has done all the ground work. He has planned and provided for every opportunity, trial, situation, and person you will face.

> Lord, I am ready to respond in my motivation
> of love and honor for you. Amen.

Prepared to Persuade, Part 2

> Because we understand our fearful responsibility
> to the Lord, we work hard to persuade others.
> God knows we are sincere, and I hope you know this, too.
> —2 CORINTHIANS 5:11 NLT

Never doubt the immense influence teachers have been given. If you ask a crowd of successful people who they credit most, besides their parents, for helping them become who they are today, most will name a specific educator.

What gives teachers such power of persuasion? The educator exhibited wisdom and compassion, and therefore the student trusted them. Students must have confidence and trust before they will listen, yield, and obey. Once that confidence is established, what educators say and do will impact students for the rest of their lives and hopefully for eternity.

The only way to prepare for this power of persuasion is to prepare every day in prayer. God has all the answers, and He is just waiting for us to inquire of Him.

Lord, I sincerely desire to work hard
to persuade others to love and follow you. Amen.

Absolutely Successful

Be strong and very courageous. Be careful to obey
all the law ... [and] do not turn from it to the right
or to the left, that you may be successful. –JOSHUA 1:7 NIV

We experienced a particularly cold winter one year. Snow piled up for weeks with single-digit temperatures and dark skies. On the first sunny day, as the snow sparkled on the ground, I saw a man riding with his convertible top down in thirty-nine-degree weather. Brrr! Later, I met someone wearing shorts.

"Aren't you freezing?" I asked.

"It's all relative," he replied. "Compared to the past six weeks, this is a heat wave!"

When comparing *cold* to *colder*, they redefined *warm*. I guess that's fine (as long as you don't get sick), but what about when we compare behavior and values? Do you hear students—or even adults—try to justify bad behavior by comparing it to other people's worse behavior? What about yourself? Do you define God's commands as absolute or based on each circumstance? We must never compare bad to worse and call bad good.

Lord, your commands are not relative to our culture.
Keep me on your absolute path to success. Amen.

Courage Can't Keep Quiet

> … a blind beggar named Bartimaeus … was sitting
> by the road. When he heard that it was Jesus the Nazarene,
> he began to cry out … . Many were sternly telling him
> to be quiet, but he kept crying out all the more,
> "Son of David, have mercy on me!" Mark 10:46-48

Jesus stopped and called for Bartimaeus to come to Him, and the attitude of the crowd went from shushing to cheerleading. "Take courage!" they said, "Jesus is calling for you!" I would like to pause here to say that I believe Bartimaeus "took courage" when he began crying out to Jesus. Bartimaeus was courageous against the reprimands of the crowd.

Their discouragement reminds me of our culture today. Our culture says, *Shush! You cannot say the name of Jesus, it is offensive.* Culture tries to blind and bind you in the chains of fear and in the captivity of its influence. But God's Word tells us repeatedly to "Take courage!"

I wonder how many people tried to shush Martin Luther King Jr.? He took courage clinging to Christ and mountains moved.

Lord, I won't keep quiet about your love
and message. Amen.

Body of Christ

If one part suffers, every part suffers with it; if one part
is honored, every part rejoices with it. Now you are
the body of Christ. –1 CORINTHIANS 12:26–27 NIV

Your classroom is a complex, connected group of people who
can stir and steer behaviors in one another. Watch as a disruptive student tries to get others to participate with them. Notice
how a class leader can persuade people to participate in projects
or give to causes.

You are a part of the body of Christ, and like the human body
you affect other parts of the body with your affection, attitude,
and actions. The human body is an amazing creation—an incredibly complicated group of cells, systems, and organs that are all
connected and working together to sustain our earthly life.

As Christians, we are the body of Christ. God has placed other Christians at your school so you can strengthen and encourage
one another. As the body of Christ on your campus, realize the
strength you have together, and use united prayer to heal the
problems attempting to infiltrate and spread.

God, may we reflect your glory as your body.
Amen.

Share the Load

Bear one another's burdens, and so fulfill the law of Christ.
—GALATIANS 6:2 ESV

When I was battling cancer, I was blessed to have many friends surround me and my family to help us bear the burdens of the battle. Many prayed, some helped with our children, others did housework, and still more brought food. I have always said, "Nothing says I love you like a casserole!" Well, okay, maybe a pie, but you get the idea. Our journey was made easier by those who joined us and helped to bear the burden of the battle and everyday life.

Do you have a testimony where someone or even a group of people rallied around you to share the load in a time of need? Maybe when you had a baby or needed to move or get your classroom ready at the beginning of the school year. God created us to care for each other; He made us for relationship with Him and with one another. We were never meant to go it alone. Who in your life needs some extra help right now, and how can you assist?

Jesus, thank you for knitting me together with friends
and family who love me. Let me be a life-lifter
for others and share their load. Amen.

Talent Scout

Now there are varieties of gifts, but the same Spirit;
and there are varieties of service … [and] activities, but it is
the same God who empowers them all in everyone.
–1 CORINTHIANS 12: 4–6 ESV

Praise God that He made us all unique with a variety of gifts, talents, and interests. What a boring and unproductive world this would be if we were all the same. Think about some of the talents that you see in your students. How do you scout out their talents and help them to work in and through those strengths? And is there room in your curriculum for them to develop and use their talents?

Realize that these are the strengths that God gave them to complete His purpose in and through their life. When you help them grow and utilize these strengths, you're helping to prepare and build confidence so that they will be successful.

God has given you special talents and strengths too. You were His idea, and He invites you and ignites you to use those talents and strengths for His glory.

> Lord, help me to be a talent scout on my campus,
> helping others recognize and grow in their giftedness
> for your glory. Amen.

Wise Teaching

Let the word of Christ richly dwell within you.
—COLOSSIANS 3:16

It is vital to use the wisdom of God's Word when teaching or giving encouragement, discipline, and especially advice. Our thoughts and ideas are useless unless founded on the Word of God. So how do we access the word of Christ in all our teaching? It must "richly dwell" within us.

The original Greek words for "richly dwell" are *plousio*, which means abundantly, and *enoikeo*, which means to influence for good or to inhabit. The only way anything can abundantly reside in or inhabit us is for us to seek it out and spend time learning it. Just like our students at test time, we cannot hope that the right answers will magically come to us if we haven't studied the material.

When I was growing up, my dad was very proud of a set of encyclopedias he bought our family. In any situation where we didn't know the answer, he would say, "Look it up." The same advice applies to us today, but with the Bible, not *World Book Encyclopedia*.

Need wisdom? Look it up!

> Lord, help me to be a wise teacher with
> your Word richly dwelling in me. Amen.

Skip the Slander

So put away all malice and all deceit and hypocrisy
and envy and all slander. —1 Peter 2:1 esv

Why do people speak slander? Some people lift themselves up by putting other people down; it's a cry for attention and affirmation. Some people want to steer negative attention away from themselves or something they did, so they smear someone else's reputation. These people are insecure and need to be introduced to repentance, forgiveness, and mercy. Gossips want us to think they're smart, informed, and in some sort of inner circle; they want to be the first to know and the first to tell. They cannot be trusted as friends or sources of correct information.

As educators, we often use words to help people. We affirm them and point out the gifts and goodness that God created in them, and we turn the conversation to another topic that can appropriately give people what they need by making them feel good about a positive attribute in their life. Choose your friends wisely, skip the slander, and be a peacemaker that speaks kindly about people.

Jesus, guard my heart and my mouth
so I please you with my words. Amen.

Delivered, Protected, and Blessed

The LORD will deliver him in a day of trouble.
The LORD will protect him and keep him alive, and he shall
be called blessed upon the earth; and do not give him
over to the desire of his enemies. –PSALM 41:1–2

I used to live on a hill with the Rocky Mountains on one side and the plains on the other. Storms blew in from all directions with gusts between twenty and seventy miles per hour, so imagine the difficulty of planting new trees that are tall and thin with shallow roots. We pounded stakes deep into the ground around them and secured straps around the trees to connect them to the posts, ensuring that no matter which way the wind blew in, the trees were protected on all sides.

Similarly, Jesus has placed posts around you to help hold you up when the troubles of life come blowing in from all directions. He posts deliverance, protection, and blessings around you, and faith, hope, and love connect and secure you to weather the winds of trouble.

Lord, may I stay securely fastened to the posts
that Jesus positions around me. Amen.

Share HIStory

Many are the plans in the mind of a man, but it is the purpose of the LORD that will stand. —PROVERBS 19:21 ESV

Shakespeare once said that the world is a stage and the men and women are merely players, but that's not true. The world is not a set, and people and things that happen are real. We experience real joy and sorrow, and life and death are not scenes. Life is not scripted, but we were born with a plan and purpose. Every day matters. Every decision, emotion, word, and deed plays out God's story.

Storytelling has great power. Think of the influence movies and television have. How would your story read if you wrote it down? Ponder that today. The greatest stories will always include people of great heart and passion—people who want to make a difference, right a wrong, heal a hurt, meet a need, teach, and touch a life with love. We are not on this earth to just survive between birth and death; we are here for a purpose—to live the story that gives God glory from our first breath to our last.

Lord, may I live your purpose
and follow your plan. Amen.

Encouragement's Everyday Effect

> But encourage one another day after day, as long as it
> is called "Today," so that none of you will be hardened
> by the deceitfulness of sin. —HEBREWS 3:13

Do you have the gift of encouragement? Do you look for ways to help someone see their value or reach their potential? As an educator, are you prone to being as excited and positive from January through March as you are the first and last weeks of school?

Everyone needs to be encouraged. Being encouraged every day has an awesome effect on your personality and performance. An effective servant running with endurance must be cheered on daily. As the writer of Hebrews points out, daily encouragement from our Christian brothers and sisters deters sin's deceitfulness; it keeps satan from getting a foothold in your emotions.

Encouraging each other daily will keep the fire burning all the way through to the last week. Your mission field awaits you, and God has surrounded you with His love and provision. Exchange encouragement with fellow believers.

> Lord, let my lips flow with encouragement
> every day. Amen.

Practice

You shall keep My statutes and practice them;
I am the LORD who sanctifies you. —LEVITICUS 20:8

My daughter loves to play piano, but she doesn't love to practice. There is a big difference between playing and practicing. Playing is leisurely and typically ignores the tricky sections or notes. Practice usually doesn't sound as good and isn't as easy. It takes time and dedication, because without practice, the tough spots we worked hard to conquer become difficult again.

My daughter learned a song perfectly, but failed to practice after she moved on to new songs. A few weeks later, she could not play the song anymore. Sternly but lovingly, her teacher said, "I do not like re-teaching songs you have already learned."

Has God ever had to re-teach you a skill or lesson because you didn't put His lessons into practice? Even tough lessons we struggle through will become dull if we don't commit to continual practice. When we learn something from God's Word or an experience, we must put the lesson into practice so it becomes our nature. Thus the saying, "Practice makes perfect."

Lord, help me to practice your lessons.
Amen.

Demonstrating God's Love

But God demonstrates his own love for us in this:
While we were still sinners, Christ died for us. —Romans 5:8 NIV

We didn't ask for Christ's love; we didn't earn or deserve it. We didn't do anything for Him first; He wasn't repaying us, and we can never repay Him. Before we were born, Jesus demonstrated His love for us.

The *American Heritage Dictionary* has four definitions for the word *demonstrate*:

1. To show clearly and deliberately; manifest.
2. To show to be true by reasoning or adducing evidence; prove.
3. To present by experiments, examples, or practical application; explain and illustrate.
4. To show the use of (an article) to a prospective buyer.[*]

In other words, a clear, deliberate example proven true through many examples and applications could result in many people who not only consume it but also reproduce it for the consumption of others. Imagine what your students might accomplish, what relationships they might attain, and what positions they could achieve if they learned these valuable life lessons from your demonstration this year.

> Lord, may I demonstrate Christ's love at all times.
> Amen.

---

[*] *The American Heritage Dictionary of the English Language,* s.v. "demonstrate," accessed February 17, 2017, https://ahdictionary.com/word/search.html?q=demonstrate.

Recognized by Love

"By this all men will [recognize] that you are My disciples,
if you have love for one another." –JOHN 13:35

By definition, *recognize* is an interesting word, and if you read its definitions together instead of as a variety of meanings, they seem to have movement. *Recognize* means to perceive, to come to know, to be known by, or to feel.

This lays out steps for us to put feet to our faith. First we perceive; we see, notice, or identify something that in turn triggers a feeling. Then, knowing the need activates us to do something about the situation, to bring love into the circumstance, even if it means making some kind of personal sacrifice. As we work to generate change, people take notice and wonder why we would care for a stranger, volunteer, donate, or fight for the rights of people we have no connection to. The simple answer is love. Along the journey we are recognized as a love-filled Christ-follower.

Jesus, thank you for letting me experience
and express your love. Amen.

Due Admiration

Do not withhold good from those to whom it is due,
when it is in your power to do it. —PROVERBS 3:27

As we sat eating at a restaurant, my daughter Emily's eyes lit up. A gasp and a squeal of glee followed as *she* walked by. *She* even said, "Hi," and waved. For the next thirty minutes, Emily kept a close watch over my shoulder, as *she* ate only a few feet away.

Emily begged to go talk to her "just for a second," but I told her to respect *her* privacy and let *her* enjoy a peaceful meal out. This was *her* personal time, and it would be impolite to interrupt. So Emily stared in adoration, almost unable to finish her lunch. I finally told Emily she could go say hello.

How do those famous stars manage to get a bite to eat without being hounded by adoring fans staring at them and approaching them to tell them how much they love them? How do they put up with that?

Well, you should know *she* was not a famous star. *She* was a third-grade teacher at Emily's school. Chances are good that you have students who feel the same way about you!

> Lord, may my actions reflect that I know
> how young eyes are watching me. Amen.

On My Knees

Come, let us bow down in worship,
let us kneel before the Lord our Maker. –Psalm 95:6 NIV

The cartilage in the knee is the thickest in the human body. It has several functions, including providing stability, lubrication, nutrition, and shock absorption. Let's think about how these relate to our spiritual lives:

- *Stability*. In the chaos we live in, with shifting circumstances, moods, responsibilities, and schedules, prayer provides the stability we need to stand firm, press on, and not fall into satan's traps.
- *Lubrication and nutrition*. We think about what we feed our earthly body, but do we consider our soul? Feed your soul with God's presence and His Word. Oil was used for offerings, anointing, and as a sign of gladness. Prayer anoints our days, thoughts, and actions to God, acting as a lubricant for any friction we encounter.
- *Shock absorption*. Prayer cushions us for the unexpected. It puts us in a place of peace, surrounded by God's care. A shocking development in our lives is absorbed and transformed into faith through prayer.

God created us to spend a lot of time on our knees in prayer.

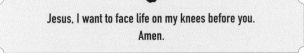

Jesus, I want to face life on my knees before you.
Amen.

Directed

Trust in the LORD with all your heart, and lean not on your own understanding; in all your ways acknowledge Him, and He shall direct your paths. –PROVERBS 3:5–6 NKJV

Do you ever get that "Oh no, what have I done?" feeling? When does it usually happen? For me, it usually occurs after I've told God, "I got this!" Failure to stop and express my dependency on Him usually results in misguided or mismanaged situations.

God brings various opportunities into our lives to discipline, disciple, and keep us dependent on Him. When we acknowledge Him, expressing a desire to abide in Him, He will direct us on the right path and prepare it for us.

What direction do you need today? Is there a student you don't know how to reach? Where do you need help making a decision concerning your job, a relationship, or a summer opportunity? Instead of thinking about the problem, focus on God and tell Him how much you need Him and want to follow His will. Praise Him, acknowledge His authority and love, and then listen for His direction.

Lord, I desire to follow your plan for my life.
Please direct me, setting me on your path. Amen.

Storyteller

The unfolding of your words gives light; it imparts
understanding to the simple. —Psalm 119:130 esv

If you've been teaching for some time now, chances are good
that you've found special ways to teach difficult concepts, making it easier for your students to grasp and master the material.

Jesus also taught deep concepts by telling stories that people
could relate to. He began His lesson on obtaining and growing
faith throughout the struggles of life by saying, "A sower went out
to sow …" (Matthew 13:3 ESV). The listeners, who were familiar with agricultural contexts, could easily relate to the spiritual
concepts of the lesson.

The art of storytelling has continued to be one of the simplest
ways to share your faith or a Bible lesson in a conversation. Being familiar with the Bible story makes it easier to share God's
Word without opening the Bible and reading it during a casual
conversation. Start gathering stories in your mind to share with
people who need encouragement, advice, or salvation. With your
students in mind, consider some contexts that you could use to
relate to their favorite app, sports, relationships, or video games.

> Lord, let your Word be on the tip on my tongue
> today and always. Amen.

Lights in the World

Do all things without grumbling or disputing; so that you
will prove yourselves to be blameless and innocent,
children of God above reproach in the midst of a crooked
and perverse generation, among whom you appear
as lights in the world. –PHILIPPIANS 2:14–15

How do your students react when you announce a pop quiz or research paper? Are you met with cheers and applause or a few groans and sighs? Even as educators, we may find ourselves less than thrilled with surprise paperwork or an added task. When this happens, pause and pray, asking God to show His hand in this opportunity to shine.

He has planned and paved the way for His purpose for you. His tasks are to grow you, not make you groan. Like your quizzes, His tests are not meant to harm you. You make plans to teach and grow your students' knowledge, understanding, and application so that their lives will be better; God does the same on a grander scale. You are set apart and challenged so that you can appear as a light in the world.

> Lord, forgive me when I complain, and help me to see
> every day as a chance to be a light for you. Amen.

February

Crowned in Love

Bless the LORD, O my soul, and forget not all his benefits …
who redeems your life from the pit, who crowns you
with steadfast love and mercy, who satisfies you with good.
—PSALM 103:2, 4–5 ESV

As Valentine's Day approaches, some people look forward to cards, candy, and a special date with their sweetie, while others dread the thought of being alone and feeling unloved. The truth is that we are never alone and certainly never unloved; God is always pursuing us and showing His love.

How do you measure the value of a relationship?

- Is it because of the amount of time you spend together?
- Is it in the way the other person listens to you or the encouragement that they pour into you, especially when you feel down and defeated?
- Is it the sacrifices they make for you?
- Is it the gifts they have given to you?
- Is your relationship strengthened by shared values and goals?
- Can you name some of the feelings they cause in you?

Now, does this sound like your relationship with Jesus? No one will ever love you more than He does.

Lord, thank you for crowning me in your love.
Amen.

Ask for His Help

But she came and began to bow down before Him,
saying, "Lord, help me!" —MATTHEW 15:25

I will never forget the first time each of my kids announced, "I
don't need your help." Ugh, painful!

It made me realize how often God must go through this same
scenario with us, or maybe just with me. How often I have run
away to complete a task I'm not nearly capable of accomplishing,
calling out to God, "I got this!" (as if He's going to be so proud
of me for taking off and doing it myself). The Spirit says, "Let
Me help," but I remain silent, working myself into a mess. God
then gives me a gentle glimpse of the chaos I have made, and I
finally ask for help and He gently restores me. Lord, thank you.
I *do* need your help!

Do you have students who think they don't need you—that
you have nothing to offer them or that they know it all? Of
course. Now think of a time in your life when you tried to accomplish something without God. What did you learn from that?

> Lord, may I always see the blessing
> of asking Jesus for help. Amen.

Hope in the Living God

> This is a trustworthy saying that deserves full acceptance
> … that we have put our hope in the living God, who is the
> Savior of all men, and especially of those who believe.
> —1 TIMOTHY 4:9–10 NIV

A few years ago, my son, Chandler, was treated for cancer throughout the year. It was a difficult time full of doctor visits, hospital stays, complications, more medications than I could count, pain, fatigue, nausea, anxiousness, and the pressing question of whether his final treatment really meant we could move on.

In looking back on that year now, I also see God's love in the faces of so many doctors, nurses, teachers, ministers, friends, family, and even complete strangers. That year, I experienced tender moments with God that I will forever treasure in my heart. Most of all, I learned that our hope is Jesus alone. I saw that this life is a vapor. In the short time we have, we cannot put our hope in anything on earth, but only in Jesus.

> Lord, I confidently put my hope in you,
> knowing that all you do is good. Amen.

Abiding Authority

My faithfulness and unfailing love will be with him, and by my authority he will grow in power. –PSALM 89:24 NLT

The first step toward a life of purpose, prosperity, and pleasure is the submissive step into the shadow of the Almighty. This vital step takes us to a place of shelter and strength, *under* the wings of God's authority. He desires to gather all people under His wings. Know that there is safety, liberty, strength, wisdom, courage, joy, hope, love, and countless other blessings under His wings; His authority is a shelter from satan's schemes and life's storms.

In addition to abiding *under* His authority, we are given the right to walk *in* His authority. Scripture describes the wisdom, power, and blessings that flow to and through those who are filled and function under God's authority. This authority is used to build up the body of Christ, not divide or destroy, and this authority glorifies God, never a person, project, or organization. It is pure of heart and powered by the Spirit.

Lord, I desire to abide in your authority,
never left exposed to the cruel elements of culture
or the weapons of this world. Amen.

Everything I Ever Did

Then, leaving her water jar, the woman went back to the
town and said to the people, "Come, see a man who told
me everything I ever did. Could this be the Messiah?"
They came out of the town and made their way toward him.

–JOHN 4:28–30 NIV

Jesus had just told a woman of her errant life with many men.
Astonished, she ran back to town and told everyone, "Come,
see a man who told me everything I ever did."

The townspeople had made this woman something of an out-
cast because of her sinful past, but everyone in that town had
secrets. It is amazing to me that the whole town flocked to see
Jesus at this woman's testimony.

I'm also amazed at this woman who, despite the harsh treatment she had received from her village, immediately ran to tell
them the best news she had. Many believed in Christ because of
her testimony, and many others believed when they saw Him for
themselves.

What amazes—and encourages—you about the woman at the
well today?

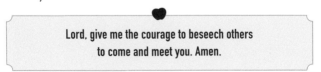

Lord, give me the courage to beseech others
to come and meet you. Amen.

Keep Your Tongue

Do not repay evil with evil or insult with insult.
On the contrary, repay evil with blessing, because to
this you were called so that you may inherit a blessing.
For, "Whoever would love life and see good days must keep
his tongue from evil and his lips from deceitful speech."

—1 PETER 3:9–10 NIV

Gossip is a deadly weapon. It can kill a reputation or a relationship faster than you can say, "Have you heard?" Rumors break trust and kill careers, yet we will sit and listen, even share them, if we think there is a valid or valiant reason.

God tells us to hold our tongue, to go to the person directly for truth, and to replace insults with blessings. We are supposed to act as a refuge for someone in pain, not expose them.

Is gossip a problem at your school? If so, pray it away. It damages students and staff. Let your lips be filled with love, never deceit.

> Lord, help me to only seek and spread truth
> bathed in your love. Amen.

Be Mine

> But you are a chosen people, a royal priesthood,
> a holy nation, God's special possession, that you may
> declare the praises of him who called you out of
> darkness into his wonderful light. –1 PETER 2:9 NIV

During this month of flowers and chocolates, we also see heart-shaped candies with messages of affection printed on them. Like candy corn at Halloween and Peeps at Easter, we either love or hate the taste of them, but we all welcome the thoughtful messages from a loved one.

The most recognized message reads, "Be Mine." If we think about it, long before we ever celebrated Valentine's Day, God sent us this same love message. But some days we distort the message to, "Be Busy." We think that God's love is based on what we do for Him, and we wear ourselves out in the name of love. We become weary while God waits for us to slow down long enough to enjoy a sunset, sit awestruck by the ocean, or just talk and be with Him.

What love message do you have for your heavenly Father today?

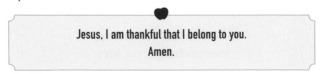

Jesus, I am thankful that I belong to you.
Amen.

Consistently Courageous

> Then he came there to a cave … and the word
> of the LORD came to him, and He said to him,
> "What are you doing here, Elijah?" –1 KINGS 19:9

The story of Elijah is one of my favorites because of Elijah's amazing faith in God. Elijah had a "mountaintop moment," calling down fire from heaven to prove that God was the one true God. In the next scene, we find him fleeing from evil Queen Jezebel and wallowing in fear in a cave. Why? Because satan does not walk away from a fight quietly.

God had shown His power in and through Elijah, yet He finds Himself asking this mighty prophet, "What are you doing here?" Faith is lived with courage and consistency, even when we think we're the only one being faithful.

As educators living out our faith, we need to know our religious rights and commit to pray, love unconditionally, and give cheerfully. We need to put on the full armor of God and fight to thwart satan.

What distractions and discouragement might be used to throw you off track? Pray and do not retreat.

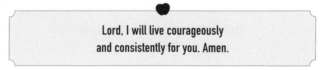

Lord, I will live courageously
and consistently for you. Amen.

Open-Book Test

All Scripture is God-breathed and is useful for teaching,
rebuking, correcting and training in righteousness,
so that the man of God may be thoroughly equipped
for every good work. –2 TIMOTHY 3:16–17 NIV

Life does not come with a syllabus; we have no idea when we
will be tested. Like a pop quiz in school, our life quizzes can
catch us unaware and unprepared, except that all of God's "tests"
are open-book. We just need to open the Bible to find what we
need.

The Bible has the answers; the reminders add to our success,
inspiration keeps us going, and correction teaches and improves
us. It includes examples of what others have learned from suffering, as well as promises to sustain and strengthen us.

If you asked your class if they wanted a closed-book or open-
book test, which would they choose? Would any of your students
opt to keep their book shut and in their desk? We face tests every
day, and leaving our Bibles shut and on the shelf may cause us
to fail.

Lord, may all of my life tests be aced by
using your book. Amen.

May the Lord Grant All Your Requests

> May the LORD answer you when you are in distress;
> may the name of the God of Jacob protect you.
> May he send you help from the sanctuary and grant
> you support from Zion. … May he give you the desire of
> your heart and make all your plans succeed. May we shout
> for joy over your victory and lift up our banners
> in the name of our God. May the LORD grant
> all your requests. –PSALM 20:1–5 NIV

I prayed these verses over you while writing this book. Praying God's Word back to Him is an excellent way to pray when we don't know someone well, what to say, or all the facts. God hears our prayers and responds to our hearts with His wisdom.

How do you feel when someone prays for you? Chances are good that it encourages you. Maybe it even increases your desire to become a stronger prayer warrior. A lot of people are uncomfortable with praying out loud. If you're one of them, don't worry about being eloquent. Just be sincere. Pray your heart, pray God's Word for yourself and others, or pray for a miracle, guidance, strength, wisdom, comfort, self-control, help, or whatever it is you or someone else needs. Just pray.

Lord, thank you for answering me in
my distress and for hearing all my requests. Amen.

Shaken to Speak

And when they had prayed, the place where they
had gathered together was shaken, and they were
all filled with the Holy Spirit and began to speak
the word of God with boldness. –ACTS 4:31

I don't know if your room has ever shaken, but I know that most teachers will be shaken at some point during the year.

As I read over the thousands of prayer requests that our ministry receives, I still shed some tears of tenderness at the loss of some of our loved ones and the terror that comes with bad news, and then I just bawl tears of triumph as I see the hand of God work many miracles and heal many broken hearts, bodies, and homes.

Look back on your life and think about the many things you prayed over–the times you were fearful something might happen and it didn't. Maybe you were anxious, and He gave you peace, or you battled, and He gave you victory. This is your testimony. These are the wonders of God that we need to proclaim boldly.

Lord, I'm inspired by how you have been faithful to me.
May I share it with everyone I meet. Amen.

Gathered

"For where two or three are gathered in my name,
there am I in the midst of them." –MATTHEW 18:20 RSV

On the way to our school one morning, I noticed a group of geese that were always gathered in the same yard. I thought, *There must be something special to draw them there*, and pointed them out to friends as we passed by. One remarked that they must get fed there and another that they must be like family or they felt protected there.

During hunting season, I saw a field of birds and hunters sitting there. Then it hit me: decoys! The geese I had seen day after day were not fed, protected, or fellowshiping in that yard; they were plastic! I prayed, "Lord, keep your church authentic, never a decoy."

We gather in our prayer groups, churches, and Bible studies, and people go by and think, *They must get fed there*, or *They must feel like family and enjoy being there*. I pray that these people come in and find real, warm worshippers with Jesus in their midst. In many parts of the world, it's not safe for Christians to gather. Many risk or lose their lives to gather for worship. May we not take that for granted.

Lord, may all your followers know the warmth
of Christian fellowship with Jesus in the midst. Amen.

Waiting to Be Well

When Jesus saw him lying there ... he said to him,
"Do you want to be made well?" The sick man answered
him, "Sir, I have no one to put me into the pool when
the water is stirred up; and while I am making my way,
someone else steps down ahead of me." –JOHN 5:6–7 NRSV

In the verses above, Jesus seems to ask an unnecessary question:
"Do you want to get well?" But he had a good reason for asking
it—to see if the man truly wanted his life to change.

Jesus asks us the same thing. Being made well is being restored to everything the Creator has for us and made us to be.
Jesus is basically asking, "Are you willing to leave what you
know—the life you have been living—and allow God to disrupt
your life by placing you wholly on His path?"

Notice that the sick man doesn't give Jesus an answer but
a familiar excuse: "Everybody pushes ahead of me, so I can't."
Excuses come from fear of change; we want to be exempt from
exercising faith and effort. Perhaps your students use the same
excuse over and over—or perhaps you do that. In what ways can
you help them (and yourself) step out and change that behavior
for the best?

> Jesus, disrupt my plans and my pain for your gain.
> I want to be whole and wholly yours. Amen.

Living Love Letters

Beloved, if God so loved us, we also ought to love one another. No one has seen God at any time; if we love one another, God abides in us, and His love is perfected in us.
—1 JOHN 4:11–12

We are living letters—signed, sealed, and delivered by God—a Valentine of sorts. No one has seen God, but they can see His love manifested in us and through us.

There are people all around us in need of the good news of the gospel and a good hug. As Christians, we have been designed by Creator God and signed with the stamp of His image. The Holy Spirit has sealed us unto the day of redemption, and Jesus has delivered us from sin, shame, and the fires of eternal torment. Commit to being a living Valentine sent to share the love of Jesus. Heaven is your return address, and you have been sent with love, to love.

Lord, may I be a love letter from you,
to everyone I meet. Amen.

Transformed

Do not conform any longer to the pattern of this world,
but be transformed by the renewing of your mind.
—ROMANS 12:2 NIV

I asked believers and some non-Christians why they opposed going to church.

Some replied that they felt like they had to *perform*, producing deep Bible knowledge or taking on numerous duties. Others said because church was just a performance, with people who acted one way on Sunday and completely different the rest of the week. Some said they didn't want to have to change or *conform* to be like everyone else at the church; they thought that joining a church meant giving up their personal identity to become a church clone. Lastly, others said, "Christians look so *forlorn*"; they believed that being a Christian meant saying goodbye to fun.

What they believed was deeply misconceived! Church is an act *of* worship, not putting on an act. As well, we are to be transformed, not conformed. Church provides opportunities for us to be refreshed, renewed, and changed for God's purpose and blessing. We rejoice because we are redeemed, blessed, and loved.

Lord, may my church and school be a place where people can come and be transparent and transformed. Amen.

Rock or Stumbling Block

"I also say to you that you are Peter, and upon this rock I
will build My church." … But He turned and said to Peter,
"Get behind Me, Satan! You are a stumbling block to Me;
for you are not setting your mind on God's interest."
–MATTHEW 16: 17–18, 23

One minute Peter was right on the mark, and the next he messed
up big time. Isn't grace an awesome thing! One minute Peter
was the rock, and the next he had stuck his foot in his mouth and
Christ was calling him satan and rebuking him. Christ admon-
ished Peter but never gave up on him.

Do you have students who can be so great sometimes but
mess up so big other times? What is your response to their great
moments and their goofs? While Peter made a big mistake, six
days later he was there for the transfiguration; Christ forgave
Peter's zealous mistake and chose to see the rock in him. Can you
do the same with your students?

Lord, may I always see the rock in others.
Amen.

212

Soul Sustainer

Behold, God is my helper; the LORD is the sustainer
of my soul. —PSALM 54:4

Many teachers have students who are part of military families, and if you do, you may find it difficult to understand how they are sustained through the extended times of separation, the anxiety of war, and the day-to-day hardships faced at home. As the child of a military member, I watched my mom suffer and sacrifice every time my dad flew off to serve his country for the sake of liberty and, in his own heart, for the Lord.

As Christians, we know full well that satan attacks where Jesus is being served. My family would battle in prayer for my dad and through the trials on the frontline and in our front yard. My mom knew that the only one who could sustain us was Jesus, so she made sure that we stayed in the Word and in church.

How do you battle against the enemy? Do hard times draw you nearer to God, or do you tend to get mad or sad and retreat from His sustaining hand? No matter what you face, take courage in knowing the Lord is the sustainer of your soul.

> Lord, draw me and sustain me
> in all my days as I give you praise. Amen.

Live, Learn, Love

See that no one repays another with evil for evil,
but always seek after that which is good for one another
and for all people. –1 THESSALONIANS 5:15

I loved my mother-in-law deeply. Early in our relationship she told me, "I had a terrible mother-in-law, and I refuse to be one, so if I ever act like one, tell me." I never had to take her up on that offer. She had experienced something painful and learned from it, and instead of repeating the pain or leaning on the excuse of, "That's all I ever knew," she refused to repay evil with evil. She chose to love instead. My frame of reference for everything she said and did was love, long before she ever said, "I love you."

How is love playing out in your life today—in your classroom, and with your family, your coworkers, and the parents of your students? In light of your past experiences, are you making exceptions or excuses when it comes to showing love? Perhaps someone loved you even when you weren't exactly lovable (we've all been there). Consider what that meant to you, and remember that grace when others treat you without love.

Jesus, help me to live, learn,
and always choose love. Amen.

Remembered and Redeemed

He remembered us in our low estate
His love endures forever. –Psalm 136:23 NIV

When difficult times come, which do you think about most—the trials or God's provision? Do you think about:

- A spouse being out of work, or still having enough money to pay the bills each month?
- Health issues, or still having the ability to work?
- Your children's poor choices, or the lesson or blessing that came out of the situation?
- Some marriage tribulation, or the stronger relationship that resulted?

Sometimes it can be tough to find something to be thankful for, even when you can recount some past blessings. When that happens, remembering His love for you can help you be thankful. Look back at His provision for you and then look forward to an unknown tomorrow with trust and faith.

> Jesus, help me to count my blessings and give thanks.
> You have remembered and redeemed me. Amen.

Psalms and Hymns

And admonishing one another with psalms and hymns
and spiritual songs, singing with thankfulness
in your hearts to God. –COLOSSIANS 3:16

I got tickled reading this verse, trying to imagine us teaching and admonishing one another with hymns. I doubt you've ever called a student to your desk by singing "Would You Be Free from the Burden of Sin," or had a student who replied by singing "Just as I Am." Have you ever started the day with "Tune Your Hearts that All May Hear" or "Trials Dark on Every Hand"? When our daughter was young, we heard her singing "Amazing Grace" while sitting in time-out.

Please do not misunderstand my humor for disrespect. Music is a great way to instruct and inspire. Think about songs that have taught you or prompted you to do something. Perhaps you could learn what inspires your students by asking them to share their favorite line of a song. Then use that knowledge to help you reach them.

Lord, I pray you would put your song
in my heart today. Amen.

Opportunity Knocks

Behold, I stand at the door and knock. If anyone hears my
voice and opens the door, I will come in to him and eat
with him, and he with me. —REVELATION 3:20 ESV

In your youth, did you ever sneak out a window? (If so, it's not likely that you were headed to church.) Did you have a moment when your heart said, "Trouble, not opportunity, is waiting outside that window"? In our youth, we often believed opportunity, not heartbreak, was outside the window, and even as adults, we make the mistake of believing that we have to manipulate or compromise in certain situations to get what we want.

What kinds of opportunities knock on windows or cause us to sneak around? Satan's set-ups! We (or our students) may think that one "shortcut" to what we really want won't hurt anyone, but if we take it, we'll stop short of God's plan. His opportunities will come to our door, not require us to crawl out a window. For the best opportunities for our life, we need to watch for open doors and keep our windows locked.

> Lord, may I always hear when your opportunities
> for me knock. Amen.

Precious Jewel

There is gold and abundance of costly stones, but the lips of knowledge are a precious jewel. —PROVERBS 20:15 ESV

You are a precious jewel, more valuable than gold! You speak knowledge into the minds and hearts of your students every day. You are giving them the information and inspiration they need, not only to earn a living but also to live out the purposes that Jesus has planned for them.

Do not shrug this off as a sweet compliment. God said these words, not me. Let this verse serve as a reminder of how wonderfully important you are in the eyes of God. Do not equate your value with the number on your paycheck or the last parent complaint you received. God refers to you as a precious jewel—prized, exquisite, treasured, priceless.

Let your voice be a valuable vault of wisdom and knowledge for all to hear, drawing them to God's plan and love for their lives.

Lord, speak knowledge into my heart, that the overflow of my lips would be precious to your kingdom. Amen.

Comforter

He comforts us in all our troubles so that we can
comfort others. When they are troubled, we will be able
to give them the same comfort God has given us.
—2 Corinthians 1:4 nlt

What are some things that comfort you? Think about some of the most comforting things that have been said to or done for you. A Scripture of encouragement, a hug, a listening ear, and buying or bringing a meal is a great way to show love and bring comfort.

How do you know when someone needs you to help comfort them? Do you wait for them to come to you and ask, or are you watchful for others in need? How can you comfort a student? Compassion and encouragement tend to be better first steps than asking, "What can we learn from this?" or saying, "You brought this on yourself." Everything from a bad day to a bad decision is an opportunity to comfort someone in the way Jesus comforts you in your troubles. Multiply His comfort; help carry their burdens and heal their hurt.

Jesus, thank you for your comfort.
Amen.

Powerless Pretending

But God says to the wicked: "Why bother reciting
my decrees and pretending to obey my covenant?"
—PSALM 50:16 NLT

My nephew loves to pretend and play dress up. He owns every superhero costume that exists, and when he pretends to be Ironman, he wants us to believe he has super powers. He wants us to fall to the floor when he sticks his palm out and makes his blasting noises. But while it's fun to play make-believe, we cannot fake faith. Like my nephew's costumes, it's nothing more than wearing a mask and making some noise. There's no real power, just pretending.

God sees our hearts and knows our intentions. He knows when we're just going through the motions during Sunday morning services or serving Him with a heart filled with love and adoration. Satan will not flee when we are pretending. He's been watching and knows if our faith is a real relationship or just "dress-up" on Sunday mornings.

There is no power in pretending; show God how real your love is for Him today.

> Lord, my love for and faith in you is real. Let my life
> reflect my heart in worship and obedience. Amen.

Nurturing News

The Spirit of the LORD God is upon me, because the LORD
has anointed me to bring good news to the afflicted; He has
sent me to bind up the brokenhearted, to proclaim liberty to
captives and freedom to prisoners; to proclaim the favorable
year of the LORD and the day of vengeance of our God;
to comfort all who mourn, to grant those who mourn in
Zion, giving them a garland instead of ashes, the oil of
gladness instead of mourning, the mantle of praise instead
of a spirit of fainting. So they will be called
oaks of righteousness, the planting of the LORD,
that He may be glorified. –ISAIAH 61:1–3

Do you know someone who is afflicted? Then bring them good
news. Do you know someone with a broken heart? Then bind
it up. Who do you know that is a prisoner, a captive ensnared
in satan's shackles of addiction, abuse, sin, or shame? Proclaim
liberty and share the path to freedom. Right now, think of someone who fits these descriptions, someone who is in need of God's
favor, justice, comfort, gladness, and strength. Who comes to
mind? With God by your side, step out in faith to make a difference.

Lord, may I be a living love letter to this world.
Amen.

Moving Mountains

And He said to them, … "If you have faith the size of
a mustard seed, you will say to this mountain, 'Move
from here to there,' and it will move; and nothing will be
impossible to you. [But this kind does not go out except
by prayer and fasting."] —Matthew 17:20–21

Jesus took three disciples up a mountain, where they saw Him
transformed in divine brightness and glory, but as soon as they
descended the mountain, chaos, a demon-possessed boy, and a
desperate father met them. The other disciples had tried to cast
the demon from the boy but couldn't. Jesus rebuked His disciples
for their lack of faith before He rebuked the demon. This sort
of "mountain" could only be moved by faith that comes from
concerted prayer.

Are you facing a mountain that needs moving, maybe with a
particularly difficult student or situation? This is when you need
prayer the most, pressing in to God to receive the faith that moves
mountains. Don't let your mountaintop experiences descend into
powerlessness, press on with faith-filled prayers so you can move
the mountains you face.

Lord, take me to the mountaintop some of the time
so I can move mountains all the time. Amen.

Dedicated

Then Hezekiah said, "You have now dedicated yourselves
to the LORD. Come and bring sacrifices and thank offerings
to the temple of the LORD." –2 CHRONICLES 29:31 NIV

A *News-Star* article once observed, "Students with parents who
are involved in their school tend to have fewer behavioral
problems and better academic performance, and are more likely
to complete high school than students whose parents are not involved in their school."*

Every one of us has a story about a teacher who showed special care or interest in us, a testimony of the impact that dedicated
teachers can make on a life. Staying devoted in our work as educators can be difficult, but this remains one of the most important
factors in our students' success. As Christians, our dedication to
our work is an extension of our dedication to God. We worship
God by serving Him in the mission field of our schools.

Devote yourself to be the best and to bring out the best in everyone around you. Dedicate yourself to success, the completion
of God's plan for your life, and the success of those He puts in
your path to help, teach, love, and encourage.

> Lord, please give me the energy and courage
> to stay dedicated to all my students. Amen.

---

* "Parental Involvement in Schools," Child Trends Data Bank, September 2013.

Significant

"The Son of Man must suffer many things and be rejected
by the elders, the chief priests and the teachers of the law,
and he must be killed and on the third day be raised to life."
–LUKE 9:22 NIV

Many things have happened in my life and I didn't grasp the significance of the event or experience until later in life. They seemed ordinary at the time, but years later brought knowledge or experience that I needed to minister, solve problems, or accomplish tasks. In today's Scripture, Jesus told His disciples the significance of what will happen, but they still couldn't grasp it until He had risen.

As educators, we get frustrated when students don't understand the significance of a lesson or appreciate the opportunities of school. Eventually everyone learns the value of school, either while they are benefiting from what they have learned or when they're wishing they had listened more and worked harder. Know that the opportunities you are providing today are valuable and will be treasured—if not today, then someday.

> Lord, help me to understand the significance
> of my past, present, and future. Amen.

March

All That You Have

And He said, "Truly I say to you, this poor widow
put in more than all of them; for they all out of their surplus
put into the offering; but she out of her poverty put
in all that she had to live on." –LUKE 21:3–4

Giving is a necessary part of an educator's job. There's the obvious giving that teachers do every day, taking extra time preparing lessons and grading homework, but there's also the gifts you help your students make for Christmas, Valentine's Day, and Mother's Day. For all these gifts, thank you.

Our verses today remind us to give to God, even out of poverty if necessary. Yes, this means from our finances, which as educators is often limited, but there can be other forms of poverty. We also sometimes feel bankrupt of time and emotional or physical energy, or even all of the above!

When we feel we have nothing left to give, God asks us to give the rest to him. In what ways can you trust him with your all?

> Lord, may I have courage to give
> out of my poverty all that I have. Amen.

Refuse Rejection

> You need to persevere so that when you have done
> the will of God, you will receive what he has promised.
> —HEBREWS 10:36 NIV

On March 2, 1904, Theodor Seuss Geisel (Dr. Seuss) was born. Thanks to him, many of us have tried green eggs and ham, have a red-and-white-striped tall hat in our classroom, and have cried more than once while reading *Oh, the Places You'll Go.*

Dr. Seuss's first book was rejected twenty-seven times before being published. If you were in his place, at what point would you have hung up your typewriter? And what would have happened if he'd decided he was not meant to write children's books?

Now think about how you respond to rejection. Whose rejection hurts or influences you the most? Perhaps you've experienced rejection from other Christians when you were seeking help, encouragement, affirmation, or even just friendship. But if God has put a purpose for His glory in your heart, refuse rejections and endure to succeed in what you know needs to be done.

May I accept others as Christ has accepted me, and
endure rejection as I pursue your purpose for my life. Amen.

Complete, Not Compete

And He gave some as apostles, and some as prophets, and some as evangelists, and some as pastors and teachers, for the equipping of the saints for the work of service, to the building up of the body of Christ. —EPHESIANS 4:11–12

As Christ-followers, our purpose, in its simplest form, is to love God and love others. All Christians are gifted by the Spirit to contribute to the completion of the body of Christ and the Great Commission. The Author of your days never intended for you to have to beat someone else out for a blessing; His thoughts and plans are specific for each follower for His kingdom.

Fellow believers are not our competition. This mind-set motivates us to truly love one another. You have absolutely nothing to lose by helping someone get promoted or obtain a grant, or by sharing your resources, because *all* you have belongs to God and has been given to you as tools for His kingdom. His plans will prevail, and you have nothing to lose and everything to gain if you help others.

> Lord, I commit to lovingly complete, and never compete for, your love and blessings. Amen.

Example

And you yourself must be an example to them by doing
good works of every kind. Let everything you do reflect the
integrity and seriousness of your teaching. —TITUS 2:7 NLT

Who did you look up to as a child? Did you imitate their behavior—the way they talked or acted? Maybe you emulated
their mannerisms? Now think about who you look up to now
and why. And think about who looks up to you. More people
than you might realize!

You are thoughtful to set an example when you are in class—
speaking directly to your students, parents, or coworkers—but as
a Christ-follower, you are also setting an example in the halls,
parking lot, and other places where you are seen and heard.
Your body language, tone, and the way you treat others speaks
volumes to those who are watching. Really, what we do speaks
louder than anything we say. Your good works reflect your heart
and character in ways that a hundred lessons or lectures could
never express.

> Lord, continue to guide me to good works
> and kind words to reflect my heart for you. Amen.

Gentleness

But let your adorning be the hidden person of the heart
with the imperishable beauty of a gentle and quiet spirit,
which in God's sight is very precious. –1 PETER 3:4 ESV

Have you ever had the pleasure of being around someone with a gentle spirit? It's not that they're a pushover or timid; they just have a calm, tender presence even in times of pressure or chaos.

Gentleness comes from faith in Jesus, walking in the shade and safety of His authority and resisting the temptation to raise our voices or compromise our witness with a biting word or hurtful reaction. Yelling at someone does not mean they will hear you any better; in fact, it is a human defense to tune out loudness. Think about your classroom. How do you get your class's attention? What is your reaction when they're loud? In moments of conflict, have you ever found strength in silence?

Praying before we speak is the best way to ensure value and volume control in our voice. It is also a guide to gentle actions, which always speak louder than words.

> Lord, I want my spirit to be precious in your sight.
> Guide me in your gentleness. Amen.

Remember

Remember Jesus Christ, risen from the dead. …
For this reason I endure all things for the sake of those
who are chosen, so that they also may obtain the
salvation which is in Christ Jesus and with it eternal glory.
—2 TIMOTHY 2:8, 10

On March 6, 1836, the Alamo fell in a predawn assault. Over two hundred men died defending the Alamo for the freedom of Texas. Despite the loss and the remaining men knowing the strength of their enemy, on April 21, 1836, the Battle of San Jacinto began with the battle cry, "Remember the Alamo!" Just eighteen minutes later the battle was over, and by the next morning Santa Anna was captured and Texas was free.

In the same way, we can remember the place where Christ fought satan for us to be free from the eternal bondage of sin, the place where He laid down His life because He would rather die for us than live without us in heaven.

When your day has gone badly, you feel you are losing the battle, the enemy seems strong and your circumstances seem gloomy, and your dream seems defeated, give the battle cry, "Remember the cross!"

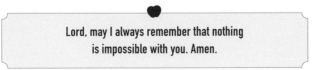

Lord, may I always remember that nothing
is impossible with you. Amen.

Called to Call

> While they were ministering to the Lord and fasting, the
> Holy Spirit said, "Set apart for Me Barnabas and Saul for
> the work to which I have called them." –ACTS 13:2

Have you ever said, "I was called to be an educator"? *Called* is the transliterated Hebrew word *proskaleomai*, and it means to bid to come to oneself. A better understanding would be the Trinity inviting you to come to Them.

Following God in this entrusted service requires us to stay close to Him. Our job is simply our opportunity to draw near and serve Him. Wisdom, strength, knowledge, patience, and everything else we need will come through Him.

"The LORD is near to all who call upon Him" (Psalm 145:18). We draw near to God when we answer His call, and He is near to us when we call upon Him. The *call* is transliterated *qara'*, which means to cry out for help. When we determine to seek Him, He is there waiting for us to invite Him to reveal Himself to us and in our circumstances.

> Lord, I will continue to follow your call,
> knowing you answer when I call out to you. Amen.

Greater Grace

Or do you suppose it is to no purpose that the Scripture says, "He yearns jealously over the spirit that he has made to dwell in us"? But he gives more grace. Therefore it says, "God opposes the proud, but gives grace to the humble." Submit yourselves therefore to God. Resist the devil, and he will flee from you. –JAMES 4:5–7 ESV

What hinders you and your students from success? Think about whether there's anything that fills the space or takes the place of God. How can you resolve to replace that space with grace?

First, we must surrender, giving up all the space in our life to the Holy Spirit. God's plans to prosper will exceed any earthly dream, but those plans may be different from what we expect. God gives greater grace when we give Him greater space in our life.

Second, we must submit. Submission means placing ourselves under the authority and control of God, yielding to and obeying Him. Unfortunately, pride likes to be our guide. Submission to the Spirit over self is a lifetime lesson, but it allows God to slam the door to satan's schemes.

> Lord, I surrender my will and my life
> and submit fully to you. Amen.

Labor for Love

"The harvest is plentiful, but the laborers are few;
therefore pray earnestly to the Lord of the harvest to send
out laborers into his harvest." –MATTHEW 9:37–38 ESV

Thank you for being a laborer for the harvest! Lest you think I have forgotten that you're a teacher and not a preacher, I would like to state for the record that you're a missionary. God has sent you into the "fields" of education, where your influence is powerful and your opportunities are plentiful. Your workplace is your mission field; God did not call everyone to be a preacher, but Jesus did command us to go and make disciples.

The world is filled with hurting people who are helpless to save themselves. You have been sent out to share His love and message. You're not here by chance; this is your mission field. Look for opportunities to tend this field as you teach and as you walk from here to there. Share His love everywhere.

> Jesus, thank you for sending me to labor
> and love for your harvest. Amen.

By What Authority

And they spoke, saying to Him, "Tell us by what
authority You are doing these things, or who is the one
who gave You this authority?" –LUKE 20:2

In this verse we find Jesus teaching in the temple, with priests
continuing to try to trick Him into saying something that will
deflate His popularity. On this day, the religious leaders had come
to question Jesus' authority. Can you imagine asking the King of
Kings where His authority comes from? The One who could
raise the dead—the One who would defeat death—was standing
right in front of them waiting for them to acknowledge all they
had seen and heard, but instead they were blinded by greed and
pride and plotted to kill Him.

You work very hard throughout the year to do what is best
for your students. How do you respond when a student or parent
questions your authority? I know it can be painful, especially if
they attack you in front of your students or on social media. But
Jesus is the ultimate authority in your life. Pause and pray that He
will guard and guide you.

Lord, help me to always live, love,
and teach under Christ's authority. Amen.

If You Love Me...

Jesus answered and said to him, "If anyone loves Me,
he will keep My word; and My Father will love him,
and We will come to him and make Our abode with him."
–John 14:23

There is nothing you or I could do to add to Christ's work on the cross. His sacrifice alone can save us. However, Jesus still makes something clear in today's verse: If we love God, we must obey His commands.

Having someone tell you they love you but then act in a way opposite to that makes it hard to believe them. Likewise, if we say we love God, our actions must prove our words true.

Obedience is a tough subject, but it is an important one. Too many studies show little to no difference between how the world lives and how Christians live. As a church, we cannot say we value or believe certain things if our actions do not follow through. Make things right within your own relationship with God and with others, then look around to see where He would have you act lovingly in His name.

Lord, may my love for you help me keep
your commandments. Amen.

Kingdom Value

"Permit the children to come to Me; do not hinder them;
for the kingdom of God belongs to such as these."
—MARK 10:14

You've probably heard a hundred times, "The future of the world is sitting in teachers' classrooms today." Future doctors, researchers, business owners, teachers, and maybe even a future president are under your care and nurture as you equip them for their destiny.

Your students' earthly futures are of great worth, but what about their kingdom value—the impact they will have for eternal purposes? How many souls might be saved through their lives? What values will they instill in their children and require of our government? And how might they change our culture or even the world from a Christian perspective?

Pray for each student by name, asking God to use you to help prepare them for His purposes. Your time with them can impact their abilities to fulfill His plans. Which characteristics would you like to nurture? There is so much more to teach than what is in our textbooks.

> Lord, may I seek and foster the kingdom
> and earthly value of my students. Amen.

Complete, Don't Complain

The soul of the sluggard craves and gets nothing, while the soul of the diligent is richly supplied. —PROVERBS 13:4 ESV

How do you approach a task that is not on the top of your "What I Want to Do" list? Are you the type of person who painfully draws out the task, hoping it will somehow magically get finished, or do you hunker down and plow through to get it over with? How much attention to detail do you give these tasks? Have you ever dreaded a task but then ended up enjoying it? Similarly, what kind of excuses do you hear from students? Do they turn in last-minute, half-hearted work, yet crave an A grade?

The truth is that we receive a blessing in every task. Perhaps we learn something new, meet someone we don't know, or get some sort of reward along the way or in a future situation. There is abundance in accomplishing all that we are asked to do to the best of our abilities. Education and experience are treasures that lead to a rich life.

Lord, help me to complete all I should
do with gladness and love for you. Amen.

The Lord Is My Shepherd: Life as a Sheep

The LORD is my shepherd; I lack nothing. He makes me
lie down in green pastures, he leads me beside quiet waters,
he restores my soul. —PSALM 23:1–3 NIV

The relationship between a shepherd and his sheep has existed for thousands of years. The shepherd watches for enemies trying to attack the sheep; he protects and provides for them. Sheep are prey animals with a strong sociable instinct, congregating close together and becoming stressed when separated. For sheep, the primary defense mechanism is simply to flee from danger. They have good hearing, and they know their shepherd's voice (see John 10:27). Sheep also possess excellent peripheral vision; they can see behind themselves without turning their heads. For this reason, they fear moving forward if something they're afraid of is behind them (see Philippians 3:13–14). No creature will lose itself sooner than a sheep, so it is apt to go astray and unlikely to find the way back.

In John 10:14–15, Jesus tells us, "I am the good shepherd, and I know My own and My own know Me, even as the Father knows Me and I know the Father; and I lay down My life for the sheep." If we follow Him, we will never go astray.

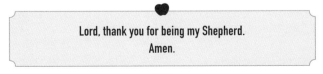

Lord, thank you for being my Shepherd.
Amen.

Prayer Pulse

And every day, in the temple and from house to house,
they kept right on teaching and preaching
Jesus as the Christ. —ACTS 5:42

As educators, our "prayer pulse" is not really any different from other vocation slants, including parent, business group, and other diverse prayer groups. The concern is not so much what American Christians are praying about, but a deep concern over what we are *not* praying about.

Just as we look for God to reveal Himself in Scripture, we need to look to God and His heart and will in our prayers. We need to pray for the lost and ask Him to give us the courage and opportunity to share the gospel with them.

If the students in our classrooms don't decide to follow Jesus, we could see the American church fade into obscurity in our lifetime—or worse, see them slip into the hands of satan for eternity. We must look to God and listen as He reveals Himself, and then make a deeper commitment to stop the lip service and begin life service.

> Lord, help me to pray mountain-moving prayers
> that delight you and fulfill your will. Amen.

Visiting Team

"Do not let your hearts be troubled. You believe in God; believe also in me. My Father's house has many rooms. … I am going there to prepare a place for you. And if I go and prepare a place for you, I will come back and take you to be with me." –JOHN 14:1–3 NIV

What is the advantage of being the home team in a ball game? Generally, your cheering section is a little louder and the field is more familiar.

As Christians, earth is not our home. Heaven is, and we are never the home team here. Satan is the "prince of this world" (John 14:30 NIV), but in the end, he will lose. Keep this mentality while you struggle and fight, especially when others sneer or boo at you for not following the crowd.

Surely you've had times when you were the only Christian in a group. Perhaps you've gone against the grain. Find other Christians who you can team up with, and cheer one another on to victory for Christ and not culture.

> Lord, I am thankful to be in your heavenly family.
> Help me to cheer on other members of your team. Amen.

Define the Relationship

"Instead, I have called you friends, for everything
that I learned from my Father I have made known to you."
–John 15:15 NIV

Have you ever heard someone use the abbreviation *DTR*? It means "define the relationship." If you teach junior high or high school, you may hear your students say it in discussing their relationships when they are unsure where they stand, usually in a dating situation. For some, the conversation is scary, while for others it is simply necessary. It sheds light on one's feelings and commitment or lack thereof.

Jesus, on the other hand, wants to clearly define His relationship with you. He wants you to be His, and He wants a full commitment. He promises to never leave you or forsake you, and His commitment is forever. Jesus will never leave you guessing if He loves you; He always has and always will!

Wishy-washy relationships are not what we need. We need steadfast love that only comes from Jesus. He wants all of you– your attention, affection, attitudes, and actions. He defined your relationship on the cross, by dying for you because He thought you were worth it.

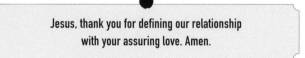

Jesus, thank you for defining our relationship
with your assuring love. Amen.

Set on the Spirit

For to set the mind on the flesh is death, but to set
the mind on the Spirit is life and peace. —ROMANS 8:6 ESV

Every day, with every breath, we decide if we trust in ourselves
or in the Holy Spirit working and breathing God's power in us.
Whether in problems or prosperity, the Spirit's response is love,
joy, peace, patience, kindness, goodness, faithfulness, gentleness,
and self-control.

The fruit of the Spirit is an outward sign that God is working
in us. It is what the world sees in our daily lives, proving that we
are different from the rest of the world. They pause to consider
our peace and confidence, and how we don't crumble under pressure but astonishingly persevere, seeking the opportunity to grow
in and glorify God with each passing pressure. Our steadfast belief that His mercy is new every morning and that He is able to
keep that which we entrust in Him is astounding.

When we set our mind on the Spirit, we have peace.

> Holy Spirit, my mind is set on you.
> Let the world see your work in me. Amen.

Confident

Therefore let us draw near with confidence to the throne
of grace, so that we may receive mercy and find grace
to help in time of need. —HEBREWS 4:16

Our confidence is in Christ alone, in our relationship with Him. It is assurance and security in Him and through Him. It is not about personal accomplishments or individual power, but is based on what Christ has done for us and not what we have done. We are confident, as we draw near to the throne of grace, that Christ was the only sacrifice that could satisfy the anger of God. Since He willingly bore our sin on the cross, we can find grace and receive mercy. Confidence shows our faith and acknowledges Christ's supremacy in our lives; we are confident in Him.

We receive help in time of need so we can in turn help others in need. The wonderful thing about sharing God's gifts is that those gifts continue to fill us no matter how much we give away. In times when we need to get or give help, we can approach God's throne of grace with confidence in Him, His abilities, and His decisions.

Lord, may I show and share confidence in Christ.
Amen.

Stronger Together

Two people are better off than one, for they can help
each other succeed. —ECCLESIASTES 4:9 NLT

Do you have a group of Christian friends to hang out with
and help one another? Maybe you regularly attend church,
a prayer group on your campus, or small group study? We are
stronger together; everyone needs at least a couple of godly
friends to learn with and lean on.

One of the most important things to do in your Christian
journey is to find a mentor who is a few steps ahead of you. Your
mentor is someone who you can ask all sorts of questions and get
biblical answers, not opinions. That person is a good listener and
encourager who you respect and are willing to listen to—someone
who will pray for you, help you find opportunities to worship
and serve God, and will call you out in love when you're making
a bad decision.

Do you have at least one mentor and one mentee in your life?
If you do, thank God for them. If you don't, ask God to help you
find them.

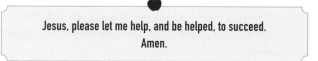

Jesus, please let me help, and be helped, to succeed.
Amen.

Teach Me

> Let me hear Your lovingkindness in the morning. …
> Teach me the way in which I should walk; for to You
> I lift up my soul. … Teach me to do Your will. … Let Your
> good Spirit lead me on level ground. –PSALM 143:8, 10

These verses express the heart of an eager student praying to his teacher. Know that you have students that long for your care and wisdom.

I once sat down with a group of Christian teens and asked, "If you could say anything to your teachers, what would you say?" Here are some of their answers:

- "If you're going to teach, show me you want to be here."
- "See me as an individual, and don't make fun of me when I ask questions."
- "If I seem distracted or depressed, ask if I'm okay."
- "Inspire me. Be the teacher I give credit to when I'm successful."
- "Let me know in some way that you're a Christian; that means a lot to me."
- "Get to know me. I might just change your life too."

Consider what your students would say if you asked the same question. Or, better yet, ask them, and then pray about how God would have you respond to their answers.

> Lord, show me the care and concern that
> each of my students needs. Amen.

No Time to Lose

Don't procrastinate—there's no time to lose.
—PROVERBS 6:4 MSG

In a mobile society or if you move frequently, it is easy to procrastinate. As a military brat and wife, I met people who would say, "When we retire … ," or "When we get to live in one place longer … ," or "When my kids are grown …" Unfortunately, they would never get involved in anything. They wouldn't commit to any cause or organization, start a hobby, or join a church. Some even refused to make close friends, knowing they were all going to move away eventually. We waste so much time and miss so many blessings by waiting for later.

What have you wanted to do or been dreaming of doing? Think about the goals you set at the beginning of the school year. I said we would revisit them, and here we are. How have you done? *What* have you done? Have you been procrastinating?

Perhaps you didn't think or dream big enough at the beginning of the school year, or maybe God has called you to do something since then that you are putting off. Recommit and remember there is no time to lose.

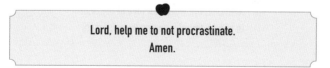

Lord, help me to not procrastinate.
Amen.

Show Your Work

If any man builds ... using gold, silver, costly stones,
wood, hay or straw, their work will be shown for what it is,
... and the fire will test the quality of each person's work.
—1 CORINTHIANS 3:12-13 NIV

As a student, I hated when teachers instructed, "Show your work." Later, I learned that was their way of determining that the students understood the process to get the solution. We don't always get to jump to the solution in life either; we need to work and pray through the process.

Every situation in life requires us to wait and trust God throughout the process, but we must work to stay the course. These are all details in our testimony: showing our work through obedience, humility, or suffering.

Like skipped steps on a math exam would detract from the answer, your testimony will not be as strong, glorifying, or meaningful if you skip a step or two. Answers are not easy, and trials give you the opportunity to show the quality of your work and the content of your faith that stands strong and pure when tested.

Jesus, let the work and love of my faith
in you be found pleasing to you. Amen.

Doing Good

And do not neglect doing good and sharing, for with
such sacrifices God is pleased. –HEBREWS 13:16

All human beings want the chance to steward their gifts well.
We all have that feeling–wanting to do something special, get
a spot on the team, or get a promotion. We want a chance, a door
opened. And for Christians, it isn't that we want to walk in the
world's applause; we want what we do to count for God and for
good.

God has given us talents and prompted our hearts for certain
things, places, and people for His purposes. We need to know
that with hard work we can grow the gifts He has given us and
accomplish the good things He has planned for us.

You have classes full of students who want this same opportunity, whether in music, sports, academics, leadership, or drama.
They have a passion to do something and for their talents to
be recognized and utilized. Encourage them to do good as they
strive to succeed.

> Lord, help me do good with the gifts
> you have given to me. Amen.

Ripening Fruit in a Rejoicing Desert

Encourage the exhausted, and strengthen the feeble. …
Then the lame will leap like a deer, and the tongue of the
mute will shout for joy. For waters will break forth in the
wilderness and streams in the Arabah. –Isaiah 35:3, 6

Not long ago, I could personally see the effects of drought as it swept through much of America. Crops withered in the ground. Wildfires raged and ravaged acres upon acres of land.

A dry and thirsty land suffers; it is not productive, but rather decays and blows away in the wind. Mankind can be like this too—exhausted, anxious, feeble, fearful, and fragile.

There will be a day when blooms cover the desert, the disabled are fully able, justice triumphs, and profuse joy breaks forth in the wildernesses of life. We can help this day come, walking with watering cans of living water and pouring out God's love and message of hope to those we meet. We must live as refreshing raindrops being poured out as an offering to our God.

Lord, use me as an instrument to bring refreshment
to a world in spiritual drought. Amen.

Hold On to Our Courage

Therefore, holy brothers, who share in the heavenly calling,
fix your thoughts on Jesus, the Apostle and High Priest
whom we confess. … Christ is faithful as a son over God's
house. And we are his house, if we hold on to our courage
and the hope of which we boast. —HEBREW 3:1, 6 ESV

Each of us faces difficulties throughout the school year, yet as
I consider Jesus' faithfulness through what He suffered, I am
inspired to persevere with courage.

Ponder for yourself what Jesus' thoughts and emotions might
have been during that final week of his life. He heard one crowd
shout, "Hosanna," and another, "Crucify Him!" He stood trial
before all sorts of authorities, yet he was (and remains) the true
Authority over everything and everyone. He never ran away,
never tried to escape. In fact, He was more concerned that His
disciples knew what was coming than He was with what He had
coming.

Our lives have many challenges, but none like Jesus'. If we
boast that we are His, then we must live as one would in the hand
of an all-powerful, death-defeating, satan-crushing, promise-keep-
ing King of Kings.

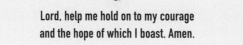

Lord, help me hold on to my courage
and the hope of which I boast. Amen.

Rely on God

For the LORD God helps me, therefore,
I am not disgraced. —ISAIAH 50:7

One morning when my daughter was six, she declared that she didn't need my help to braid her long hair that fell past her hips. Though I knew she would need my help, I let her try, hoping this would turn into a good lesson.

It did, and not just for her. When I couldn't wait any longer before the bus would come, I finally entered her room to find her with more knots in her hair than a Barbie doll that had been stuffed in a drawer for months. Still, she wouldn't let me touch her hair until I finally had her look in a mirror, and she only then allowed me to gently brush out all the knots.

Then I realized how often God must go through this scenario with us. We want to accomplish something without Him, not realizing how deeply we need Him. Finally, and only when He gently shows us the mess we've made, we let Him help us.

Oh, that we would simply remember how much we need the Lord!

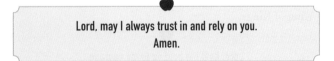

Lord, may I always trust in and rely on you.
Amen.

Lighten the Load

"Come to me, all you who are weary and burdened,
and I will give you rest. ... For my yoke is easy
and my burden is light." –MATTHEW 11:28–30 NIV

Evaluate your yoke right now. Think about all of it: errands, appointments, social obligations, children's activities, church, clubs, homework projects, classes, Bible study, e-mail, housework, prayer/quiet time, company, sports, hobbies, work, and every other responsibility. Now I want to ask you, if God spoke loud and clear to you right now and told you what He wanted you to do, where would you fit Him in? God reminds us that in all our commitments, His yoke is easy and His burden is light.

We all frequently have opportunities to take on more commitments instead of saying no. Everyone is vying for our time. Before saying yes to anything, ask God what He has for you in this season. Ask Him to guide you to the opportunities that help you and your family accomplish His mission for your lives. Then say no to the rest, because God's yoke is easy.

Lord, help me to not overstuff my load
as you lead me in your mission. Amen.

Real Relationships

He who loves purity of heart, and whose speech is gracious,
will have the king as his friend. —Proverbs 22:11 esv

We were made for relationship, so it's not surprising that one of the biggest distractions on our campuses is the search for a "real" boyfriend or girlfriend. As early as preschool, students begin talking about "liking" someone. As they move to middle and high school, the circumstances get more serious as students believe that they need to have someone who is not *just* a friend; having a boyfriend or girlfriend becomes a defining characteristic of their worth.

Real is not when someone uses another to make someone else jealous, to get help in some way, or to get physical and then walk away, but we see all this play out with our students and possibly our coworkers throughout the year. How can we help them?

Discuss with students the need to *be* real in all relationships. Friends, bosses, coworkers, teachers, and others can only relate and react to the person they see in front of them, so make sure the person they see is *you*.

Lord, may I have, and help others build,
real relationships. Amen.

Wisely Wait, Walk, and Watch the Will of the Lord

For once you were full of darkness, but now you
have light from the Lord. So live as people of light!
For this light within you produces only what is good and
right and true. Carefully determine what pleases the Lord.
—EPHESIANS 5:8–10 NLT

As much as I enjoy springtime, I always dread the decisions that must be made concerning what programs and jobs will be cut in the upcoming school year. But instead of looking at your situation as an attack, look at the craziness, confusion, and challenges as God's opportunity to glorify Himself. This simply becomes a chance for you to wisely wait on, walk in, and watch the will of the Lord.

We must trust God and be the light that exposes dark deeds. These days are opportunities for us to do His will, walk in His ways, and be His witnesses. We have no idea what the future brings, but God has prepared us and the path. Celebrate and congratulate those who are promoted, and carefully consider what pleases the Lord.

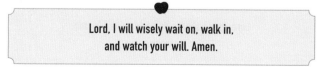

Lord, I will wisely wait on, walk in,
and watch your will. Amen.

Do as Jesus Did

"If I then, the Lord and the Teacher, washed your feet,
you also ought to wash one another's feet. For I gave you
an example that you also should do as I did to you."
–JOHN 13:14–15

As educators, we know the best way to teach is to walk our students through the process a time or two so that they can see how it's done. Jesus seemed to have that same teaching style, lovingly demonstrating the lessons and giving examples in relatable ways for deeper understanding and application.

In the passage above, disputes about greatness continued to plague the disciples' conversations and hearts despite three years of lessons. Jesus girded Himself, grabbed a towel, and bowed down on the floor to wash their feet. He finished the lesson by saying, "Do as I did to you." Servanthood was the lesson plan of the day.

Have you been asked to do something that you felt was "beneath" you? As a veteran teacher, are you insulted when assigned a responsibility usually given to a first-year teacher or a teacher's assistant? Never miss the opportunity to bow down so God can lift you up.

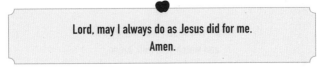

Lord, may I always do as Jesus did for me.
Amen.

April

Showers of Blessings

I will bless them and the places surrounding my hill.
I will send down showers in season; there will be
showers of blessing. —EZEKIEL 34:26 NIV

The saying, "April showers brings May flowers" is not just an agricultural lesson; it is a life lesson. This saying is used to encourage us to endure the soggy and stormy days with the promise of beauty on the other side.

Rain has many contributing factors, such as temperature, pollution, and environment. In areas where pollution builds up during the week due to business and commuters, there is actually a higher chance of rain on Saturday than on Mondays. As we sin, pollutants build up in our spiritual lives. God may choose to send a storm, as He did with Jonah, to persuade us back under the umbrella of His authority.

Do not ever believe that all storms are a result of sin. Some come to bring God glory like when Jesus walked on the water. Still others are a result of living in an imperfect world with imperfect people. Always look for the blessing in the storm and the beauty on the other side.

Lord, send your showers of blessings
and I will praise you in the storms. Amen.

Christ's Endurance

> Let us also lay aside every encumbrance and … run with
> endurance the race that is set before us, fixing our eyes on
> Jesus … who for the joy set before Him endured the cross
> … and has sat down at the right hand of the throne of God.
> —HEBREWS 12:1–2

Jesus endured the cross because His heart was set on the joy of reuniting the Father with His fallen children. I pray you feel that joy as you remember Christ died for you. As His arms were stretched out on the cross, He embraced us with the endurance of love that would stop at nothing.

Spring can be filled with many opportunities for us to endure for the joy set before us: our students' growth, success, promotion, or even graduation. These last few months are challenging—full of state and national testing, school ratings, and funding—and jobs hang in the balance.

Endurance is needed, because the difference you make in students' lives is important—the classroom is your mission field. He has everything in His hands, and He loves you.

Lord, thank you for your love as I walk
and work in your example of endurance. Amen.

Go with Me

"Go up to the land flowing with milk and honey.
But I will not go with you, because you are a stiff-necked
people and I might destroy you on the way." ... [Moses
said,] "If you are pleased with me, teach me your ways
so I may know you and continue to find favor with you.
Remember that this nation is your people."
The LORD replied, "My Presence will go with you,
and I will give you rest." –EXODUS 33:3, 13–14 NIV

Were you ever so exasperated with your class that you couldn't even walk down the hall with them because you weren't sure what you might say or do? In the above verses, God was so fed up with Israel that He told Moses He would not accompany them to the Promised Land because He might destroy them on the way. If you think you have a challenging time with those around you, talk to God; He will understand.

Thankfully, the Israelites repented. Moses reminded God that these people were not his but God's. Finally, God agreed to go with them. Your students are His children; let that help you keep your perspective.

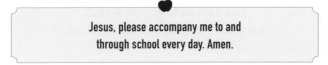

Jesus, please accompany me to and
through school every day. Amen.

Satisfying the Crowd

Wishing to satisfy the crowd, Pilate released Barabbas
for them, and after having Jesus scourged, he handed
Him over to be crucified. —MARK 15:15

Wishing to satisfy the crowd. These are such dangerous words. Pilate had plenty of reasons *not* to harm Jesus. He knew the chief priests were envious of Jesus and that they had worded the charges against Him to infer He was a political rebel. But Jesus didn't have an army, and even His closest followers had scattered. Despite all this and a warning from his wife, Pilate chose to satisfy the crowd of priests and handed Jesus over to be crucified.

Spring can be a dangerous season for our students. Spring break, prom, and graduation often lead to "crowd-pleasing" bad choices with life-changing and even life-ending consequences. Pray for all students through this season—that those who have worked hard for thirteen years to get into the best colleges will not make tragic mistakes because they want cheers from their peers, and that relationships will not be lost. Pray that following Christ will be their priority over popularity.

> Lord, please protect me and my students from
> trading our destiny for popularity. Amen.

Gifted

In his grace, God has given us different gifts
for doing certain things well. –Romans 12:6 NLT

What is the usual response you get when you compliment someone? What is their response when you tell them they have a "gift" or that they're "gifted"? God has created everyone to be "gifted" at something to help equip them for His plans.

Scripture tells us to use our gifts for God and through God. Culture, on the other hand, spends most of its time and money focusing on and trying to overcome weaknesses. While it's important to learn basic skills and to grow abilities, success comes when we operate in our strengths. Most successful people develop their strengths and develop relationships with people who excel in the areas where they are weaker.

Sometimes people are resistant to believing that they have a certain talent or ability. What do you think causes people to ignore or to hide their gift? Now think about yourself. Do you know what your gift (or gifts) are? How are you using them for God's glory?

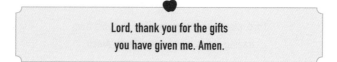

Lord, thank you for the gifts
you have given me. Amen.

Anything, Lord!

Now it came about after these things, that God
tested Abraham, and said to him, "Abraham!" And he said,
"Here I am." He said, "Take now your son, your only son,
whom you love, Isaac, and go to the land of Moriah,
and offer him there as a burnt offering." —GENESIS 22:1–2

God tested Abraham's faith in Genesis 22. In the original Hebrew language, when God called to Abraham, Abraham answered, "Anything, Lord." Before he knew what God wanted or was going to say, his obedient greeting to God was a promise of a blank check—*anything*.

We know the rest of the story. God sent Abraham to Mount Moriah to offer his one and only son as a sacrifice. Abraham went, knowing God had made a promise and that He always kept His promises. By faith, Abraham would do the unthinkable—the impossible—knowing God was in control.

Isaac was spared, with God providing a ram in his place. We were also spared, with God providing Jesus in our place. Offer God a blank check; anything and everything!

> Lord, my heart's reply to you is,
> "Anything, Lord!" Amen.

Heart and Hope

I pray … your heart may be enlightened, so you know …
hope of His calling … riches of the glory of His inheritance
in the saints, and … the surpassing greatness of His power
toward us who believe. —Ephesians 1:18–19

These verses act as a prayer as we embark into new opportunities of glorifying Christ. We have been called to a mission field: imparting the next generation with information, inspiration, and application. Being an educator is a vital mission to not only equip students with book knowledge but also to influence them about God's calling on their lives. We are more than teaching a subject; we are modeling abundant life.

We are at war with every force fighting against what Jesus offers, but we are also equipped for this with His power. He has authority over every malevolent force, and evil flees at the faith-filled spoken name of Jesus.

Every day, focus your heart on the surpassing greatness of His power that you walk in. Be filled with hope, and let Jesus be glorified as you teach and touch those at your school.

> Jesus, enlighten my heart with the hope of your
> calling and your surpassing greatness. Amen.

Godly Guide

The righteous is a guide to his neighbor.
—Proverbs 12:26

It can be difficult to determine when to step in and when to step back when it comes to guiding your students. Maybe you see them making snap decisions that you know they'll regret, and you wonder how you, as an educator, can encourage or advise them. Do you feel like you have that option, or do you feel like your hands are tied when it comes to giving life advice? Do you think your students follow or remember your guidance?

The good news is that research shows that students *are* listening when you're talking to them. In a variety of polls over the years, a teacher or staff member at a school was given credit as "most influential," or a close second, only surpassed by a parent, in a person's life. Your students are not only guided by what you say to them, but also what you do, how you do it, and why you do it.

> Jesus, thank you for the influence to guide my students
> and others in your wisdom and ways. Amen.

Disciplined

"Those whom I love, I reprove and discipline; therefore …
repent. Behold, I stand at the door and knock; if anyone
hears My voice and opens the door, I will come in to him
and will dine with him." –REVELATION 3:19–20

Discipline is a multifaceted subject; it can bring to mind sweet lessons learned as well as places we never want to return to. Discipline is meant to be administered with love, in love, and to bring lovable results. Jesus follows His statement of discipline with love and His desire to have an intimate relationship. When you discipline your own children or students, you don't want them to pull away in anger but listen and grow.

Sadly, many people have suffered abuse. Abuse is not love, and it is not acceptable. Never confuse God's discipline with abuse. He loves us so much, more than we can understand. Let His discipline draw you closer to Him to protect and grow you in wisdom. "All discipline for the moment seems not to be joyful, but sorrowful; yet to those who have been trained by it, afterwards it yields … righteousness" (Hebrews 12:11).

> Lord, I desire to always experience
> and accept your discipline in love. Amen.

Life More Abundantly

"The thief comes only to steal and kill and destroy;
I came that they may have life, and have it abundantly."
–JOHN 10:10

One year, my Bible study discussed the medical horror of crucifixion. One of the men present said emotionally, "I would have never asked Jesus to do this for me!"

God gave me insight into this statement, as just a few days before, my son had been so sick from his cancer treatments that all he could do was groan in his bed. I sat with him, fighting back tears, and told him, "If I could take this cancer for you, I would do it in a heartbeat!"

Later, I thought about what I would expect my son to do if I could take his cancer for him so he could have a healthy life. Simply put, I would expect him to live life to the fullest, making the most of every opportunity, and not waste a moment. I would want him to really live!

That's what Jesus wants for us. He suffered through our torment so we could have abundant life. Let's live it.

> Lord, thank you that you give me life,
> and life more abundantly. Amen.

Living

> I have been crucified with Christ. It is no longer I who live,
> but Christ who lives in me. And the life I now live in the
> flesh I live by faith in the Son of God, who loved me
> and gave himself for me. —GALATIANS 2:20 ESV

As Christians, we must remember that we serve and worship a *risen* Savior who died for us and now lives. Jesus emerged from the tomb fully alive, not as a ghost but as a walking, talking, eating, touchable, living risen Savior. Forty days later He ascended to heaven, where He continues to live, and sent the Holy Spirit to live in us. The tomb was empty, but we are full.

Christ modeled, and called us to live, a life that draws others to Him through a life of prayer, care, and sharing His message of salvation. Our lives are a walking testimony; our prayer for ourselves and others, our care and compassion for our neighbors, and the hearing of the good news is a lifestyle of love and obedience. Live for Him as lovingly and unselfishly as He lived and died for you.

Jesus, live in me and through me.
Amen.

Blessed in Stress

Dear friends, *do not be surprised* at the fiery ordeal that
has come on you. ... But *rejoice* inasmuch as you participate
in the sufferings of Christ, so that you may be overjoyed
when his glory is revealed. If you are insulted because of the
name of Christ, *you are blessed,* for the Spirit of glory and of
God rests on you. ... However, if you suffer as a Christian,
do not be ashamed, but *praise God* that you bear that name.
... So then, those who suffer according to God's will should
commit themselves to their faithful Creator and continue to do good.
—1 PETER 4:12–14, 16, 19 NIV

How do you respond to stress? Read the verses again and pick
out the responses:

- *Do not be surprised.* We are imperfect people in an imperfect world.
- *Rejoice.* We have the opportunity to learn and glorify Christ in us.
- *You are blessed.* We are and will be blessed.
- *Commit yourself to God.* We must focus on Him and follow His Word.
- *Continue to do good.* We must continue to do the righteous thing for the righteous reason; we should pray, persevere, and praise.

Lord, help me to remember that
in times of stress, I am blessed. Amen.

Cultivating Faithfulness

> Do not fret because of evildoers, be not envious toward
> wrongdoers. ... Trust in the LORD and do good; dwell in
> the land and cultivate faithfulness. –PSALM 37:1–3

Spring semester can be an emotional rollercoaster for educators. The worst part of it is when districts begin the process of deciding which programs and teachers they will keep and which ones they will cut. I have seen many team-spirited, close-knit schools turn into war zones during these stressful weeks of staffing decisions.

Today's Scripture gives us a twofold lesson that can help even out the rollercoaster road trip of spring semester. First, it tells us the wicked who scheme and do evil will wither away. Second, it encourages the righteous to trust God to establish them.

I pray fervently that this unrest does not happen in your school, but if it does, God promises to be trustworthy. Rest in Him, no matter what wicked and hurtful things are done around or to you. He will see you through it all.

> Lord, thank you for helping me cultivate faithfulness,
> knowing fully that you say I reap what I sow. Amen.

Blood Donor

This is my blood of the covenant, which is poured out
for many for the forgiveness of sins. —MATTHEW 26:28 NIV

I needed blood for my surgery and was asking a friend to pray for me as we walked in the school hallway. As we passed my daughter's teacher, Mrs. Murphy, she asked what we were discussing and I explained.

"I wish I could help you, but I have a rare blood type," she responded. "It's A negative."

"That's what I need!" I exclaimed.

Mrs. Murphy looked at me with the sweetest expression and said, "You can have it all—every drop!"

This inspired me to picture God preparing to create the earth and all its inhabitants. I could see him discussing with Jesus how free will and pride would lead to sin and the need for a Redeemer. I could almost hear God say, "Son, I am going to need some blood," and Jesus reply, "You can have it all—every drop!"

Christ left His throne in glory to come to earth and suffer an excruciating death so that we might live forever, and heaven's gates opened wide as His blood was shed on the cross.

Jesus, thank you for being our heavenly blood donor—
our source of eternal life. Amen.

Completely His

> For the eyes of the LORD move to and fro throughout
> the earth that He may strongly support those whose
> heart is completely His. —2 CHRONICLES 16:9

God is not only watching you; He is watching *out for* you. Following Him is not a leap into some unknown, but a step into the light that He has already prepared.

The word *completely* is the transliterated Hebrew word *shalem*, meaning full, perfect, covenant relation. Your responsibility is to keep your heart completely His, not partitioned off in pieces.

Scripture says God gives us strong support in return for our heart. *Support* is the transliterated Hebrew word *chazaq*, meaning to strengthen, make firm, become mighty, and prevail. Have you ever felt a little weak or felt the ground shaking under your feet? No matter what, God is your firm foundation. He has you in His grip and will never let you go.

He formed your heart, and He is certainly worthy of the emotional overflow of it. The greatest gift you could ever give would be giving your heart completely to God.

> Lord, my heart is fully yours every day.
> Amen.

Fear of God

The LORD your God directed me to teach you to observe
… so that you, your children and their children after them
may fear the LORD your God as long as you live by keeping
all his decrees and commands that I give you, and so that
you may enjoy long life. –DEUTERONOMY 6:1–2 NIV

The fear of God is not a fleeing kind of fear but a respectful, submissive response to Him and His mightiness.

Consider how you want your students to "fear" you—to be respectful and to follow your rules. You want them to acknowledge your authority over them and trust your wisdom and knowledge to teach and lead them. You do not want them to argue with you, deceive you, or think that they know better or more than you do.

At the same time, you want a relationship with them. You want them to trust you and to feel safe in your class. They should come to you when they need help and ask questions and participate in class. You want them to know that you care and that they matter deeply to you.

> Lord, I fear you with great love and respect.
> Amen.

Meditate on God

On the glorious splendor of Your majesty and
on Your wonderful works, I will meditate. –Psalm 145:5

Meditation is all the rage these days, as doctors, celebrities, and business people sit still, clearing and calming the mind, taking a deep breath and tuning out the noise and chaos around them for a few minutes. For thousands of years, Jews and Christians have called this our preparation for prayer. God calls His people to "be still" (Psalm 4:4). Having a quiet time each day is not the end of our prayers or focus on God; it is the beginning of the discussion and dependency on Him.

Mantra meditators chant, "Om," believing it brings peace, protection, and abundance to a person. As Christ-followers, we must be careful not to confuse and combine God's prescribed practices with the world's counterfeit distractions. We meditate on His Word, ways, and will. We think about His attributes and affection. We rest in His sufficiency and grace. And we pray words of admiration and gratitude as we rest in His ability and willingness to guide and guard us so that His purposes are fulfilled in our lives.

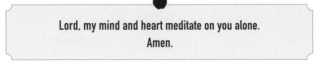

Lord, my mind and heart meditate on you alone.
Amen.

Sent out Not to Settle

The LORD said, "Behold, they are one people, and they all
have the same language. And this is what they began to do,
and now nothing which they purpose to do will
be impossible for them." –GENESIS 11:6

God had commanded Noah's family to scatter, repopulate, and become the nations of the earth. But as the generations and centuries passed, we see at least two major sins committed in these passages (sins that still plague people today).

The first sin was disobedience; God told them to "scatter," but they decided to "settle." God had the whole earth for them to explore, experience, and populate, but they decided to settle for one plain. The second sin was pride. The tower of Babel represented their belief that they could reach heaven by their own hand and their own means. They had everything on their side: God's instruction, God's promises, unity, and clear communication. Yet they looked to themselves.

Imagine for a moment what could be done on our campuses, in our communities, and throughout the world if we were committed to hearing and obeying God, and if we could communicate clearly and were united for the destiny God had ordained.

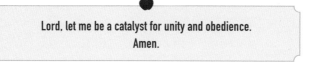

Lord, let me be a catalyst for unity and obedience.
Amen.

Identify

> Now these things happened to them as an example,
> and they were written for our instruction, upon whom
> the ends of the ages have come. —1 Corinthians 10:11

Sometimes we can identify with the character, actions, or relationships of people as we study the Bible. I can often identify with the disciple Peter, who loved Christ profusely but let his zealousness get him in trouble. Do you have any students like that?

Christ was patient with Peter. I can imagine Jesus thinking, *Here we go again,* as Peter called out, "Lord, if it's really you, tell me to come to you, walking on the water" (Matthew 14:28 NLT). Jesus loved Peter and knew his kingdom value and purpose. He was loving, correcting, and forgiving toward Peter, which prepared Peter to be a leader in the early church.

This gives me hope as I ask forgiveness when I blow it. God knows my heart for Him and His purpose for me. Now it is your turn. Who do you most identify with in the Bible and why?

Lord, may I find examples and
instruction in Scripture. Amen.

Walk in Prayer... Everywhere!

Pray continually. –1 THESSALONIANS 5:17

O h, if only I didn't have to clean, cook, tend to my home, and fulfill all my responsibilities, how I would love to spend all day, every day, on my knees before God!

This is what I used to think this verse commanded me to do, yet I now recognize it's impossible. Thankfully, God taught me to walk in prayer–literally, prayer walking! God does not desire for us to spend our entire life in solitude, head bowed and eyes closed, although there is a time and place for that type of prayer too. God's desire is for us to pray our way through each day.

While prayer walking can be done simply as you go about your day, it can also be done by targeting somewhere specific. You can prayer walk a government building, neighborhood, city, meeting place, business, church, or school. Wherever you prayer walk, simply invite God to be present there and ask for His protection, blessing, wisdom, strength, and guidance in that place. You can also do this in your school, claiming the whole campus for God and asking Him to show you where you can be part of the blessing He has for that place.

Lord, thank you that I can walk
in prayer–everywhere. Amen.

Reference Your Source

He is the source of your life in Christ Jesus,
who became for us wisdom from God, and righteousness
and sanctification and redemption, in order that,
as it is written, "Let the one who boasts, boast in the Lord."
—1 Corinthians 1:30–31 nrsv

In school, we teach how imperative it is to thoroughly give credit where credit is due on a bibliography page for information, definitions, stories, Scriptures, statistics, and so on. Failure to reference a source is plagiarism, also known as stealing, and claiming the glory and credit for something written by someone else is not only a crime but also a sin. It would be like sharing an idea that you have been working on with a coworker and then having them share it at a staff meeting as their idea. Would you ever do something like that?

You probably said no, but we all do this when we forget to praise, thank, and acknowledge God for equipping us. We may get a promotion or a grant, have a smooth parent-teacher conference with the world's most difficult parent, or turn a student's life around from certain disaster. The list goes on and on, and all credit and glory go to Jesus.

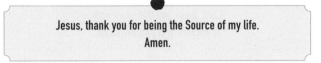

Jesus, thank you for being the Source of my life.
Amen.

The Good Work

And I am certain that God, who began the good work within you, will continue his work until it is finally finished on the day when Christ Jesus returns. –Philippians 1:6 NLT

In the above verse, Paul is certain of these comforting things:

- His own confidence
- Confidence in God
- The good work
- Work within us
- His work
- Completed work
- That Jesus is coming back

The good work is salvation, attained by believing in the good news and believing we do not merit saving. While salvation is a one-time yes to God, it is also an ongoing process; our role is to surrender and allow His Holy Spirit to work in us.

We are to be faithful to our calling and representing Christ, which will show His hope within us. This completes the "work of education" in students; we give a future and a hope He has given us. We have all heard it, but it's good to be reminded that our students don't care how much we know until they know how much we care.

Lord, I trust you to complete the work you began in me, and may I complete your work in my classroom. Amen.

Showers of Speech

"Let my teaching drop as the rain, my speech distill
as the dew. … For I proclaim the name of the LORD!"
—DEUTERONOMY 32:2–3

April showers bring May flowers, as the saying goes. Spring rains water previously sown seeds to bring growth. This is true for not only physical growth but also spiritual growth.

I've challenged you to see yourself as a living love letter from God, to ask God who needs a message of encouragement and love from Him and then make sure you delivered it. Revisit today the seeds you have planted through being a living love letter.

How can you water those seeds again to help bring growth? Just like with our students, it is not enough to just know the subject; we are only successful teachers if our students can apply what they know. In the same way, we must grow in Christ, not simply know Him. We must add wisdom and understanding to our knowledge.

In what ways can you help others grow in Christ through love?

Lord, lead me to those you want to reach,
so I can shower them with loving words
that grow and teach. Amen.

Bite to Bucket

> When the woman saw that the tree was good for food,
> and that it was a delight to the eyes, and that the tree was
> desirable to make one wise, she took from its fruit and ate.
> —Genesis 3:6

Genesis 3 records satan's conversation with Eve in the garden of Eden. He tempted her by introducing doubt and making her think that God was depriving her of something desirable. Eve took the bait when she took the first bite.

My friend shared this same type of perspective in her battle to lose weight. She resolved that God and dieting did not deprive her, but that weight loss and better health was going to be a gift from God. When she went to the movies and smelled the popcorn, she heard the tempter's voice say, "Just take a bite." And as she reached for a few pieces, she heard the voice say, "Just eat the bucket." How quickly satan tries to move us from bite to bucket!

What lies have you fallen for? What ill-fated bait do you see your students taking? And how do you mentor those who are in so deep that they can't see their way out? In all things, go to the Father for wisdom.

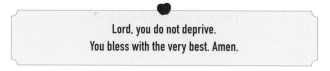

Lord, you do not deprive.
You bless with the very best. Amen.

Timeless

There is an appointed time for everything. And there
is a time for every event under heaven. –Ecclesiastes 3:1

Shortly after the tan and rest from spring break wears off, right around state and national testing time, teachers start counting the days on the calendar until summer vacation. It's not a reflection that we don't like our jobs; we simply look forward to time with our families, working around our house, and possibly even getting some rest.

Calendars include our schedules, appointments, and travel; they remind us to do things and meet needs and deadlines. But God does not operate by our calendar.

Once I wanted to post my next doctor's appointment on God's calendar with the prompt, "Heal Kathy before this date." God had a more glorifying timeline. Bills come due, but blessing you with riches may not be on God's to-do list by the first of the month. While we may pray for things to happen by a certain time, we must trust God to know best and appoint the right time.

Lord, may I trust your timetable and
may my prayers be timeless. Amen.

Knit Together

That their hearts may be encouraged, being knit
together in love, to reach all the riches of full assurance
of understanding and the knowledge of God's mystery,
which is Christ, in whom are hidden all the treasures
of wisdom and knowledge. –COLOSSIANS 2:2–3 ESV

God has knit together a wide range of needs and personalities in your hallways and classrooms. You may have one student who can't stop thinking about her prom dress and another who only owns one pair of jeans. Some have parents who are sick, in jail, on drugs, or living a less-than-model lifestyle for their kids. One student's biggest problem might be a pimple while another's is that he has to work two jobs to help feed his family. Some may worry about college, while a few have already given up on their future.

One thing they all have in common, though, is that you're their teacher. Be encouraged. God has knit you into the fabric of their lives; it is beautiful and complicated at the same time.

Lord, I pray for educators who have more
complicated classrooms than I, and I thank you for your
beautiful fingerprints all over every student. Amen.

Footprints on the Waves

And He said, "Come!" And Peter got out of the boat,
and walked on the water. —MATTHEW 14:29

Look back on this year and think about your prayer requests and how God answered. Think about the days or weeks you didn't think you would survive but God carried you through. Consider the challenges you didn't think you would overcome and yet an answer, perhaps even a miracle, broke through and left you awestruck by God's unexpected answer.

These are the moments when you look back, that if you look close enough, you notice something different about the storm. Look closely and you'll see your footprints on the waves! The storm was different for every school and educator, but at some point this year Jesus called you to come out to Him in the storm and you got out of the boat and walked. The storm squalled, the wind blew, and the circumstances tried to sink you, but you kept your eyes on Jesus and left footprints on the waves. Never forget how that felt.

> Lord, I remember how those days and waves felt. I remember your voice, hand, and answers. Thank you! Amen.

Learn to Discern

> Then I sent a message to him saying, "Such things as you are saying have not been done, but you are inventing them in your own mind." For all of them were trying to frighten us. —NEHEMIAH 6:8–9

Not everyone was happy about Nehemiah rebuilding the wall. Three troublemakers sent false messages, attempting to distract and destroy him, but Nehemiah discerned that each message was false and followed God's call to finish the work set in his heart.

It's important that we be able to discern the voice of God and godly counsel from worldly advice full of selfish motives and destructive criticism. To do this, ask yourself the following questions:

- Is there unresolved sin in my life that I need to deal with? If yes, then confess and repent quickly. If not, satan is accusing where there is grace, heaping guilt where there is only forgiveness.
- Is the person's advice biblical? Can they show you Scripture to back up their advice or confirm your decisions?
- Is the person's motive glorifying or self-gratifying?

This is the communication age, and you and your students have messages coming at you from all directions. Be sure you know who is doing the talking.

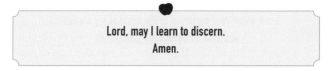

Lord, may I learn to discern.
Amen.

Intentional Instruction, Observable Objectives

I instruct you in the way of wisdom and lead you
along straight paths. When you walk, your steps
will not be hampered; when you run, you will not stumble.
—PROVERBS 4:11–12 NIV

Writing lesson plans includes justification of each lesson, project, and activity with matching, concise state objectives. We need to have prescribed purposes to our plans, and observable results. The state has decided what every child needs to learn during that grade, and as teachers we have to prove that we are making progress toward the goals.

God intends for us to walk and work out the wisdom we obtain. There should be an observable, maybe even measurable, change when wisdom clears the path to success. If we expect intentional instruction and observable outcomes, then we need to define the destination. What is "success"? How will students know which way to go if they don't know where they want to go?

Having dreams and goals is important at every age, even if they change now and then. Ask your students *who* they want to be, not just *what* they want to do.

> Lord, plant your purposes in the heart of my students,
> and lead us down your path. Amen.

Taking Off

Lift up your eyes and look to the heavens.
—ISAIAH 40:26 NIV

The sign on the classroom door read, "Taking off for summer." It meant classes were finished, but my mind wandered. "Taking off" brought images of a launching—a celebrated beginning, not an ending. A rocket launches after years of construction, research, education, experiments, decisions, training, and more. Does this sound like anything you're familiar with?

You have spent the year doing all these things. You're launching students to the next level of education, or perhaps launching seniors to work or college. It is an exciting time of new adventures—a beginning, not a stopping point.

Take a chance, stretch, and do something you've always wanted to do. Write a book, take a class, create something, try a new hobby, skydive, climb a mountain, or go on a mission trip. The sky's the limit! God gave us this big, amazing world with breathtaking sights to see, wonderful people to meet, and magnificent things to taste! There are scholarships, grants, and sponsors out there to help, and God loves to see you grow.

> Lord, let's begin the countdown to summer
> and "take off" together! Amen.

May

Made Complete

Finally, brethren, rejoice, be made complete, be comforted,
be like-minded, live in peace; and the God of love and
peace will be with you. –2 CORINTHIANS 13:11

May is finally here. For some of you, June cannot come soon enough. These final weeks can be trying and emotional. What are your biggest challenges during this part of the year?

Complete is the Greek transliterated word *katartisis*, meaning a strengthening, perfecting of the soul, disciplining, or instructing. God began a great work in you at the beginning of this year, and as promised, He saw you through with blessings, tests, victories, and holidays. In these last weeks, I beg you to press in, encourage one another daily, and live in love and peace.

You have been surrounded by many witnesses, watching to see how you will handle the tough times and tougher students. Remain steadfast and comforted as God takes this opportunity to strengthen, discipline, and instruct you, making you complete for such a time as this.

> Lord, I rejoice as you equip me to complete this school year,
> knowing your love and peace are with me. Amen.

Finish Strong

[Jesus prayed,] "I glorified You on the earth,
having accomplished the work which You have
given Me to do." –JOHN 17:4

Christ knew His days on earth were drawing to an end. God had sent Him here with specific tasks—an exact purpose—and now, having accomplished His work, Christ was preparing for a strong finish.

As the school year is ending, are you on track or scrambling to get everything done that is required? Are these last days fun or a nightmare? For some of you, the answer might be, "Both," depending on the moment. The worst days were yet to come for Jesus; He knew what He had to do and did it for you. Maybe there is something you still need to do—something hard or even painful—but it must be done.

Ask someone to pray for you in these last days—for the emotion of saying goodbye, the exhaustion, the worry over what did not get done, and the eagerness for what will be. I pray that you accomplished much, and as you count down the days to a well-deserved break, you are also preparing for a strong finish.

> Lord, help me to finish strong.
> Amen.

One Nation under God

Blessed is the nation whose God is the LORD.
—PSALM 33:12

In 1808, Thomas Jefferson wrote in a letter, "Fasting and prayer are religious exercises. The enjoining them an act of discipline. Every religious society has a right to determine for itself the time for these exercises … and this right can never be safer than in their hands, where the Constitution has deposited it."*

Since the first call to prayer in 1775, when the Continental Congress asked the colonies to pray for wisdom in forming a nation, the call has continued through our history. In 1952, a joint resolution by Congress, signed by President Truman, declared an annual National Day of Prayer, and it was later signed into law by President Reagan.

Use the days surrounding the National Day of Prayer to recall and teach the many ways that our founding fathers sought the wisdom of God when facing critical decisions. Our nation needs prayer, and we ourselves all need prayer. Pray for our nation and proclaim Jesus as the God of our nation. Pray as the Spirit leads you.

> Lord, we are one nation under God. May we live up to our motto with our laws and lives. Amen.

---

* "Thomas Jefferson to Rev. Samuel Miller," *University of Chicago,* accessed February 21, 2017, http://press-pubs.uchicago.edu/founders/print_documents/amendI _religions60.html.

National Day of Prayer

And [if] My people who are called by My name humble
themselves and pray and seek My face and turn from their
wicked ways, then I will hear from heaven, will forgive
their sin and will heal their land. –2 CHRONICLES 7:14

The first Thursday in May is the National Day of Prayer. Waves
of prayers are lifted up from dawn to dark on behalf of our
nation. How pleasing this must be to our heavenly Father, to hear
the multitude of prayers.

The National Day of Prayer is a day to humble ourselves and
praise God. We seek Him earnestly–His ways, His heart, and
His character. It is a day of repentance, when we confess and turn
from our sin, as well as seek new beginnings, forgiveness, and
healing. Thousands of prayers are said for educators, students,
and districts across the United States.

On this day, people will gather at flagpoles and in federal
buildings, cafés, and churches. People will be on their knees in
hotel ballrooms and office meeting rooms, on beaches and mountain tops. Will you join us?

> Lord, show me who I can pray with on
> this special day of prayer. Amen.

Endure

> We count those blessed who endured. You have
> heard of the endurance of Job and have seen the outcome
> … that the Lord is full of compassion and is merciful.
>
> –JAMES 5:11

When have you been put to the test? What have you had to endure this year? Perhaps you have seen the fruits of your labor as your students learn and mature. Or maybe your most trying struggles have not been with students; maybe they have been with your administration, district decisions, or even personal trials. Know that your pain is not in vain!

You may not get to see great change in your students, but you have planted seeds. Do *not* give up! Soak in the reward as past students come by to visit you and God gives you a peek at their progress.

These last few weeks are precious, and they will pass by so quickly. You are probably tired and ready for summer. You may feel that you don't have much more to give–but God does. When we work, we work; but when we pray, God works. There is still work to be done.

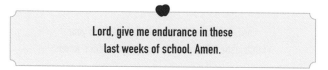

Lord, give me endurance in these
last weeks of school. Amen.

A Peter Transformation

Peter said to them, "Repent ... be baptized in the name of
Jesus Christ for the forgiveness of your sins ... Be saved
from this perverse generation!" ... Those who had received
his word were baptized; and that day there were added
about three thousand souls. –Acts 2:38, 40–41

At Pentecost, Peter was transformed from a man who was
known to, in his enthusiasm, stick his foot in his mouth, into
a courageous leader who preached boldly and followed in the
footsteps of Jesus. From the moment Jesus saw Peter, Jesus knew
the treasure of purpose He had placed inside Peter as he was
formed in the womb.

We all have had a "Peter" in our classroom—a student full of
enthusiasm who took us to the brink of frustration almost daily.
These children are filled with God-given potential, and, with a
great teacher, can be transformed from class clown to class president.

You are following in the footsteps of Jesus, the greatest teacher
of all. With prayer, patience, and good preaching, your "Peters"
might just change the world.

> Lord, enable me so I can help transform your
> enthusiastic followers into equipped leaders. Amen.

Going Through

Jesus was going through all the cities and villages,
teaching in their synagogues and proclaiming the gospel
of the kingdom, and healing every kind of disease
and every kind of sickness. –MATTHEW 9:35

Jesus was a busy teacher, but He was never too busy to care. His schedule was never too full to be compassionate or to act where there was a need. As Jesus was going through His day, He prayed, cared, and shared the love and message of God.

One day as Jesus was on His way to raise a daughter from death, the faith of a woman reaching out for His robe stopped Him in His tracks. Interruptions filled with faith did not annoy Him but gave Him joy to glorify the Father.

You can follow in His footsteps by praying, caring, and sharing His love and message as you go through your day—as you drive to school, walk in from the parking lot, and walk to and through the halls, cafeteria, gym, office, classrooms, and lounge. Watch for those in need of a helping hand, an answer, or encouragement, then stop to meet their need.

> Lord, may Christ's love go out through me
> as I go through my day. Amen.

Gardeners

"You know the saying, 'One plants and another harvests.'
And it's true." –JOHN 4:37 NLT

You are a gardener in God's kingdom. Sometimes you get to
sow the seeds; other times you pull some weeds. You may
get to nurture and water what has already been planted by other
teachers, mentors, or parents, helping it to grow stronger. Once in
a while you get the blessing of seeing the fruit, and you know that
many moments and mentors were involved but only God causes
growth and the harvest.

Seeds are planted every day in many ways. You may feel like
you haven't made a difference in anyone's life, but the truth is
that you have planted a beautiful orchard that will sprout and
bloom and one day give God great glory. Keep this in mind as
you go through your day. Plant some seeds and pull some weeds,
and keep the pests off the fruit and the enemy out of the orchard
with prayer and discipline. Enjoy watching your students sprout
and bloom.

Lord, thank you for causing fruit in my life.
Help me to plant and nurture a harvest for you. Amen.

Intercessors, Not Critics

For God did not send the Son into the world to judge
the world, but that the world might be saved through Him.
–JOHN 3:17

Hollywood deeply influences your students; the film and television industry is the biggest influence of culture. It inspires them, and shapes their dreams, how they live, what they value, and what they aspire to be and do. Arts and entertainment influence our decisions too–how we vote, serve, spend money, and treat people. Just imagine what the other six centers of influence would look like if Hollywood was transformed by the love and character of Christ!

Fear grips Hollywood's people. They wonder how long will they last, and if they will win an award, get a call to work, or have enough money. But true love casts out fear. We cannot expect those who don't know Jesus to behave like virtuous, Bible-believing Christians. And how will they know Him if we don't go with compassion, instead of criticism, and tell them–or better yet, show them. For God so loved Hollywood that He gave His one and only Son. Hollywood needs more intercessors, not critics.

Lord, fill Hollywood with your presence.
I pray their influence glorifies you. Amen.

Finish the Race with Grace

"However, I consider my life worth nothing to me,
if only I may finish the race and complete the task the
Lord Jesus has given me—the task of testifying to the
gospel of God's grace." —ACTS 20:24 NIV

Paul knew that prison and hardships faced him as he pressed on toward Jerusalem, yet nothing could hinder him from going. He even considered his life worthless if it was not on the road to finishing the race and completing the task Jesus had given him.

The last weeks of the school year can be very challenging. The race is not over; there are still lessons to be taught, projects to turn in, and papers to grade. There are also many opportunities to pray for students as they make life-altering decisions, both good and bad.

During all this, pray that your class is filled with laughter and that you have made progress on the goals you set. As the shepherd of your classroom flock, set your sights on the task God has given you.

> Lord, help me finish the race with grace.
> Amen.

Share Your Story

Listen, my son, and be wise, and direct
your heart in the way. –PROVERBS 23:19

I was blessed with an amazing mother-in-law. Daphne was born and raised in England during World War II, then married a handsome Air Force man who moved her far from home and all she had known.

I loved spending time with her, listening to the stories of her life. She was intelligent—a life-long learner who could share great details whether talking about her own life or a subject she was studying. She was also intentional; she never wasted a day, taking opportunities to travel, see shows and movies, go out with friends, and spend time with family. She kept her mind and body fit, and her love for rescuing terriers kept her life and house full of wagging tails and long walks. I learned so much from her over hundreds of cups of tea.

Who do you lovingly pour your life's lessons into? As a teacher, chances are good that you've had a number of students who you've been a role model or mentor for. Take heart in knowing that your love, encouragement, and wisdom can change their world and put them on the path to knowing their Father who loves them deeply.

> Lord, prepare my heart to listen to
> and share life's stories. Amen.

Father Knows Best

For your Father knows what you need before you ask him.
—MATTHEW 6:8 NIV

While standing outside a store on Mother's Day weekend, a little boy was earnestly explaining to his dad how much his mommy would like a puppy for Mother's Day. The little guy was very persuasive, giving several reasons why a puppy was the perfect gift. The dad listened but then said no; he knew best despite the child's desire and debate to get a puppy.

Have you ever asked your heavenly Father for something for yourself, or even in intercession for someone else, and the answer was no? Was your response, "Father knows best"? God always knows best; He knows all the facts and the future. We don't need to lay them out for Him as if we might have a bit of information He's missing. He knows our heart's desires and our weaknesses, and He knows what will benefit us and what will break us.

What if your students asked you to never give them homework or tests? Would they benefit from that request? We don't always benefit from what we want either.

Father, you always know and give what is best.
Amen.

Learn to Listen

The eyes of the LORD are toward the righteous and
his ears toward their cry. When the righteous cry for help,
the LORD hears and delivers them out of all their troubles.
—PSALM 34:15, 17 ESV

Students sometimes say that they have tried to talk about important issues and decisions but don't feel like they were heard. Have you felt that way before, expressing concerns or challenges only to have someone try to finish your sentences or start a lecture before you even completed your thought? Perhaps you avoid people who try to fix things before you finish speaking.

God listens attentively to our prayers. His help is based on our invitation for Him to intervene in our situations. Listening is an important life skill; it waits attentively and hears the heart as well as the words. Listening includes a silent prayer that invites God to talk and give us wisdom and discernment. Listening expresses respect and compassion; it opens the door for trust and future conversations. Listeners get to speak wisdom based on all the information, not on an opinion based on interruption.

> Lord, thank you for listening for my cries
> and being attentive to my prayers. Amen.

Urgent

Preach the word, be urgent in season and out of season,
convince, rebuke, and exhort, be unfailing in patience
and in teaching. –2 TIMOTHY 4:2 RSV

Do you know anyone who has been given a second chance at
life? Maybe they were healed of a terminal disease or escaped
a terrible accident or the consequences of a bad decision, and
now they live with a new outlook and appreciation for life, relationships, and responsibilities. They take advantage of opportunities quickly and live more adventurously, not wanting to miss one
sweet moment. Life is precious and we cannot count on tomorrow; we should therefore make the most of every day.

You too have been given a second chance. We were all terminal, headed for the gates of hell, and then in one heart-filled
decision to trust and follow Jesus, we were swept into eternal life
and now walk with new inspiration and conviction. Make the
most of every opportunity; let love be the theme of your days and
faith be the joy in your steps. Live life urgently, and teach others
of God's love as if there is no tomorrow.

> Lord, let me live life and love urgently
> every day. Amen.

Firmly Planted

How blessed is the man who does not walk in the counsel of the wicked, nor stand in the path of sinners, nor sit in the seat of scoffers! … He will be like a tree firmly planted by streams of water, which yields its fruit in its season and its leaf does not wither; and in whatever he does, he prospers.

—PSALM 1:1–3

What is your reaction when you see a "good" student begin to hang out with a group of students who are often in trouble? You can quickly see changes in the fruit when there is trouble at the root. As educators, we have been trained to watch for changes in a student's circle of friends, but our own circle of friends is just as important.

Yes, Jesus was known for talking and dining with sinners, and we should follow in His footsteps. But those were people He was ministering to, not his closest friends. Jesus' friends were the disciples with whom He walked, worked, and fellowshiped.

God has planted you near people who will lift you up and walk with you in righteousness. Instead of letting social pressures lead us into groups that distract us from God, we must stay focused on Him, and so become fruitful trees for His glory.

Lord, plant me firmly as I delight in your Word with trustworthy friends. Amen.

Strong Attraction

Draw near to God and He will draw near to you.
Cleanse your hands, you sinners; and purify your hearts,
you double-minded. –James 4:8

The magnet on our refrigerator strongly held up a beautiful photo of the mountains. However, the magnet was not able to hold the photo, my daughter's picture, a note from my son, and a cartoon from the newspaper. So was my refrigerator no longer attracting the magnet? Of course not. We simply put too much between the magnet and the refrigerator.

This is similar to our attraction to God; when we are most focused on Him, we prioritize our closeness to stay connected. But as we put things between ourselves and God, we lose the strength of the attraction just like that poor overworked magnet on my refrigerator.

We didn't put all that stuff under the magnet at once; it accumulated over time. Can you relate? You join something, say yes to a committee, volunteer here, have to go there, and you end up skipping church, missing prayer, and losing your connection.

What is filling the space between you and God? Is there something you could eliminate?

> Lord, I desire a strong attraction to you.
> Let nothing come between us. Amen.

Shine Bright

And those who are wise shall shine like the brightness of the sky above; and those who turn many to righteousness, like the stars forever and ever. –DANIEL 12:3 ESV

We are all on a journey through life trying to make sense of our situations while searching for significance. It's been said that "The two greatest days of your life are the day you were born, and the day you figure out why."

We were all born with a purpose. Being an educator is an essential part of your purpose; it is the passion in your heart that allows you to soar over the classroom chaos and district drama with peace and persistence. You work hard and persevere to reach your goals and ultimately fulfill your purpose. Your journey is not easy—far from it—but with Jesus you are equipped in magnificent ways to live a fulfilling life even if the culture around you seems empty and dark. You shine like a light in the darkness, and you soak up Christ's love and share it, shining it into the lives of your students, coworkers, and community.

> Lord, help me to shine so that others
> will see you. Amen.

Change, Challenges, and Crisis

"Blessed are you when people insult you and persecute you,
and falsely say all kinds of evil against you because of Me.
Rejoice and be glad, for your reward in heaven is great;
for in the same way they persecuted the prophets
who were before you." –MATTHEW 5:11–12

Many will recognize today's Scripture as a portion of the Beatitudes. As a Christ-follower, we have to decide, or resolve, that we are going to choose righteousness. In every decision, every thought, and every action; we must make every effort to think, say, and do what is right according to God's Word.

This doesn't mean we're perfect, but it does mean that we're committed to a standard of doing the right thing–always! Christians should be committed to doing the righteous thing, without fear of man or earthly consequences, because we are focused on kingdom impact and eternal consequences. We would rather offend man than God, and we would rather be unpopular or even unemployed rather than be deemed unfaithful.

Lord, I resolve to behave as I profess to believe,
knowing in obedience I am blessed. Amen.

Know Better, Be Better

Guard your steps when you go to the house of God.
To draw near to listen is better than to offer the sacrifice of
fools, for they do not know that they are doing evil.
—ECCLESIASTES 5:1 ESV

An acquaintance of my family did something very inappropriate and offensive. When I said to my son, "She knows better than that!" he responded, "I doubt it." And he was probably right. She was not being raised in a Christian home; in fact, her misbehavior mirrored that of her household. She had never gone to church, prayed, or heard God's Word. So how could she know better?

You have friends and students who also don't know God or anything about Him. Pray for them. You may know someone who knows *of* God but doesn't really understand that He has a plan and provision for their life. If so, please tell them. Perhaps you know someone who knows and professes to love Jesus but is not living the life He desires and commands. Share Christ's love and message so they not only *know* better but also have a chance to *be* better.

Lord, I listen to know you more.
Please help me be better. Amen.

The Right Stuff

And I will teach you the way that is good and right.
But be sure to fear the LORD and serve him faithfully
with all your heart; consider what great things he
has done for you. –1 SAMUEL 12:23–24 NIV

On May 5, 1961, Alan Shepard became the first American in space. The first US human spaceflight mission, named *Freedom 7*, represented the seven Project Mercury astronauts, later deemed "The Right Stuff." The objective of Project Mercury was to determine man's capabilities in a space environment and in those environments to which he would be subject upon going into and returning from space.

Take a moment to consider what the students you taught this year will accomplish in their lives. Your objectives are similar to Project Mercury's. Much of what you have done this year will determine capabilities in a school environment and in the environments your students will be subject to. That's quite a mission!

You've passed through rigorous training and testing and met stringent requirements to accomplish goals and change lives. God has given you the right stuff to be an educator.

Jesus, thank you for the great things you
have done for me and through me. Thank you for
teaching me what is good and right. Amen.

Sending Encouragement

Encourage the exhausted,
and strengthen the feeble. —Isaiah 35:3

I enjoy looking at posts on social media to see and hear what my friends and family are up to. Social media has become an amazing way to share life's milestones and prayer requests, watch children grow up, and, of course, to see what everyone's eating for dinner. Our culture shares everything!

We live in an exhausted society. Ask someone how they are doing and chances are they will say that they're tired. In the spirit of today's Scripture, I have a one-day, one-week, or even one-month challenge for you. I challenge you to write a card, e-mail, text, or social media message to at least three people, telling them how much they mean to you, how they have touched your life, something special about them, or some other form of encouragement. Instead of writing to others about you, simply write to others about them. It doesn't have to be long, just sincere.

Lord, show me the people in my life
who need encouraging. Amen.

Powerful Prayers

Rejoice always; pray without ceasing.
—1 Thessalonians 5:16–17

Wrapping our hearts and minds around who God really is and what He is capable of is impossible for us as finite individuals. God wants us to trust that He is all that He says, and to believe that He loves us in a way far beyond anything we can imagine. With these two things in mind, please allow me to challenge you to increase the power of the prayers in your prayer life:

- *Relational.* Do your prayers express relationship? Do your heart and words express love, trust, and obedience?
- *Radical.* Are your prayers based on the need for the one true God to move mountains? Are your thoughts God-sized or weak and whiny?
- *Revealing.* Are you asking God to reveal Himself and to glorify Himself? What are you revealing about your heart and thoughts about God in this prayer?
- *Responsive.* Are you being responsive and responsible for what God has asked you to do and believe? Has He prompted you to do something but you haven't obeyed? Do you really trust God enough to respect His response as you pray relational, radical, or revealing prayers?

Lord, I desire to pray powerful prayers.
Amen.

Never Thirst

Jesus answered, "Everyone who drinks this water
will be thirsty again, but whoever drinks the water
I give him will never thirst." –JOHN 4:13-14 NIV

I enjoy coffee. When I taught Bible study, a friend (the best teacher's pet ever!) brought me coffee before every class. One week she brought me a cup with two straws sticking out of the top. I tried to drink out of the straws, but nothing came out. The cup was warm and heavy, but nothing would come through my straws. I pulled on the straws to make sure they were not stopped up, and the straw (it was only one straw) popped out; it had been bent in half to distinguish my drink from hers. The straw was not submerged in the source of what was sweet and satisfying. With both ends of the straw in my mouth, I was left thirsty and disappointed.

No matter how many trips we make to the world's "well," we'll remain thirsty as if drinking from a bent straw. Only Christ gives living water.

Jesus, I come to drink deep from you,
my Designer, Definer, and Deliverer.
In you, my cup always overflows. Amen.

Extra Eyes

I pray that the eyes of your heart may be enlightened in
order that you may know the hope to which he has called
you, the riches of his glorious inheritance in his holy people,
and his incomparably great power for us who believe.

—Ephesians 1:18–19 NIV

As an educator, having an extra set of eyes might be a great
help. Today's Scripture says that we do have an extra set of
eyes—the eyes of our heart. Some translations call them "the eyes
of your understanding." Have you ever learned something new
and felt like your eyes were opened by it? This implies significance and a desire to apply it. It is never enough for us to just
introduce a concept to our students; they must practice and apply
it for progress and success.

Opening the eyes of our heart means seeing God's plan in
places and people when others might miss it. It also means perseverance when others might give up, faith when others are in despair, peace in chaos, patience instead of frustration, solutions for
problems, and, most importantly, a closer relationship with God.

Lord, open the eyes of my heart
so I know your hope and power. Amen.

Unforgettable

Let all that I am praise the LORD; may I never forget
the good things he does for me. —PSALM 103:2 NLT

Do you remember your first day on campus as an educator? Whether it was recently or decades ago, chances are good that you remember the excitement and the butterflies in your stomach. Do you recall your goals and the thoughts that filled your heart and mind as you stepped into the school? Now think about the number of students that have passed through your life and how you have touched and changed their lives.

When students from past years come back to visit you, they're saying, "You have a special place in my heart" or "I haven't forgotten how important you are to me." They're continuing to hold you and what you taught them close to their hearts. Their visits may be inconvenient as you rush around trying to start or end your day, but stop and take the time to soak up the appreciation, love, and respect. You are unforgettable!

Lord, may I never forget all the good things
you have done. Help me and my lessons to
be unforgettable to my students. Amen.

Missed Blessing

I will hasten and not delay to obey your commands.
—Psalm 119:60 NIV

One day, I pulled cookies out of the oven and called to my son, Chandler. He ran through the kitchen and headed right for the basement without stopping. He thought I was going to tell him we needed to run errands or do something he didn't want to or that he might've done something I didn't approve of. Chandler's mind was set on playing, and he hoped I wouldn't call him a second time. Meanwhile, there sat the warm chocolate chip cookies on a napkin, just waiting to bless him.

This made me think about how we can ignore God's calling and prompting in our lives. We think He is asking us to do something or go somewhere we don't want to go, not really considering that He has prepared a blessing for us there. Or we act deaf because He might be discipling or redirecting us and we have our mind set on what we want, but in the process, we miss a far better blessing in the other direction. Let's keep this in mind the next time we hear our Father's call.

Lord, hasten me to your calling,
knowing it always ends in blessings. Amen.

Act Now

"Seek the LORD while he may be found;
call upon him while he is near." –ISAIAH 55:6 ESV

Graduation is not a one-day event; it is the celebration of thirteen years of hard work. Every morning bell signals the opportunity to know and grow more, and every afternoon bell indicates a step closer to graduation. For most students, it resounds with dreams, hopes, and encouragement that you and dozens of other teachers have poured into them.

The success or failure of each student depends on how closely they pay attention and how diligently they ask questions and soak up your teachings for the ten months they're in your classroom. You make yourself available—perhaps offering, nudging, or even insisting that they spend extra time with you and their books—but the decision to do so is ultimately theirs.

Today's verse is a warning and a promise, a counsel and a comfort. It is the beseeching invitation and reminder to call upon God, because He is near, while preaching the ominous reality that the heavenly clock ticks a countdown to expiration—a final bell.

> Lord, shape and sharpen my focus
> on you each day. Amen.

Sacrifice

And walk in love, as Christ loved us and gave himself
up for us, a fragrant offering and sacrifice to God.
—EPHESIANS 5:2 ESV

Sacrifice. This word conjures up a variety of definitions and examples: "I sacrificed sleep to watch my favorite show"; or "I sacrificed my Saturday to help my friend move"; or "I sacrificed half my lunch because my coworker forgot hers."

Real sacrifice is more than giving up a few hours of sleep, a time of recreation, or half of a sandwich. Sacrifice involves pain, significant loss, and an emotion or devotion behind every selfless act. Tears, and oftentimes blood, is shed. Jesus' ultimate sacrifice provides the path to be perfected, at peace with God and eternal life for all who would call upon Him as Lord and Savior.

The sacrifice of the lives given by military men and women throughout the centuries has provided priceless protection and freedoms beyond understanding. We must remain thankful for the sacrifices that have been made to give life and liberty.

Lord, thank you for the sacrifices that have been
made so that we can live in faith and freedom. Amen.

Beautiful Heritage, Rich Inheritance

> The lines have fallen to me in pleasant places;
> indeed, my heritage is beautiful to me. –Psalm 16:6

As saints, we dwell securely in the knowledge that Jesus has overcome the grave. Our beautiful heritage prompts our thoughts to the pleasant places that God has led us to and through and encourages us to keep God continually before us so that we cannot be shaken.

This type of trust only comes from a correct knowledge of the heritage of our faith and the One in whom we trust. We have to know the history of God's power and faithfulness to know the richness of our inheritance to come.

It's up to us to share the story of his glory so that others can dwell securely and joyfully in His presence and pleasures forever. Sadly, many school curriculums have wrongly rewritten the history and faith of our founding fathers, whose driving desire for religious freedom made them willing to risk their lives to come to a land where they could freely worship God as they chose. Thank God today for your beautiful heritage and its security in Him.

Lord, thank you for giving me boldness
to carefully and academically teach the beautiful
heritage and rich inheritance of my country. Amen.

Building Memorials

> Cornelius, a centurion … who feared God … gave many alms to the Jewish people and prayed to God continually. … [The angel] said to him, "Your prayers and alms have ascended as a memorial before God." –Acts 10:1–4

Cornelius, a Gentile, was a devout man of God. He was generous to Jews, and they respected and appreciated him despite their religious culture viewing him as an unclean outsider … until an angel came.

The angel told Cornelius to send for Peter to come and minister. As Peter spoke, the Holy Spirit fell on the Gentiles, just as He had on the Jews at Pentecost. God's heart for "all to come to repentance" (2 Peter 3:9) collided with the "memorial" of prayers spoken by a Gentile who loved God deeply, and it changed the destiny of countless other Gentiles who would believe and be saved.

What memorials have you been building in prayer? There is no expiration date on your prayers; they will outlive you, your students, and their children. Once they leave your lips, they stand forever as a fragrant memorial before God, long after your memories fade.

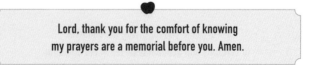

Lord, thank you for the comfort of knowing
my prayers are a memorial before you. Amen.

Meditate on His Word

This book of the law shall not depart from your mouth,
but you shall meditate on it day and night, so that you
may be careful to do according to all that is written in it;
for then you will make your way prosperous,
|and then you will have success. –JOSHUA 1:8

God gave us His Word to reveal Himself as the one true God throughout the generations. The Bible gives us a history of His faithfulness and love, and He also uses it to communicate His boundaries that protect, provide for, and guide us in what we should do. He gives us a glimpse of the past and future. Most importantly, Scripture tells the redemption story; Jesus is the eternal story, and His message and ministry fill the pages of the Bible.

Meditating on Scripture is essential for our heart and mind. Our thoughts can wander, and discouragement, distractions, and disappointment can sneak or charge in and disrupt our thoughts and days. Choosing a verse, multiple verses, or chapter to read, meditate on, and memorize gives us an anchor to bring our thoughts back to truth and steadfastness.

> Lord, I will meditate on and obey your Word.
> Amen.

June

A Good Read

You show that you are a letter from Christ, the result
of our ministry, written not with ink but with the Spirit
of the living God, not on tablets of stone but on
tablets of human hearts. –2 CORINTHIANS 3:3 NIV

What have you read lately? A short tweet or a long novel can pull you into another person's world. It can fill you with compassion, anger, or hope, influencing your actions. Today's verse refers to us as living letters, written with the Spirit of God for the world to read.

So what message do we carry? When someone "reads" us, what do they learn? Are we a love letter, a message of hope, an instruction booklet? Do we live lives that inform and inspire?

Fill your life's "love letter" with words of encouragement or inspiring quotes when you send out assignments, resources, and reminders. Guard what you post on social media. Ask yourself, "Is this glorifying? Will it help those who read it see Christ in me?" Post love, hope, faith, and joy. Let the world be drawn into His Word when they "read" you.

Lord, let my life be your masterpiece,
a living love letter and a good read. Amen.

Abounding With...

Now in Joppa there was a disciple named Tabitha
(which translated in Greek is called Dorcas); this woman
was abounding with deeds of kindness and charity
which she continually did. –Acts 9:36

Tabitha was well loved in her community and loved her community well. Scripture tells us that she was kind and charitable to many, so much so that there was a plea for Peter to come when she fell ill and died. How wonderful to be thought of in such a way that your community or campus feels that they cannot go on without you.

If this verse was written about you, what would it say?

Now in (your town), there was a disciple named (your name) who was abounding in (your attributes), which he/she continually did.

Think about where you make your mark. What are you known for, and what do students and coworkers say about you? Have fun with this activity, keeping it positive and encouraging. Feel free to even be a little silly. I picture Jesus as a man of many smiles and laughs.

> Lord, I desire to abound with deeds that meet many
> needs and plant seeds wherever you lead. Amen.

Giving

> But Peter said, "I have no silver and gold, but what I do
> have I give to you. In the name of Jesus Christ of Nazareth,
> rise up and walk!" … and immediately his feet and
> ankles were made strong. —ACTS 3:6–7 ESV

You are wealthy whether you realize it or not. While it is true that educators are not paid nearly what they deserve, you are filled with worth. Like Peter, you may not have any silver or gold to give out, but you still have a lot to give. In this instance, Peter's bold faith and Spirit-filled gifts allowed this lame man to get up and walk.

You come across people who are limping through life every day. Some have had their legs knocked out from under them, and they don't have the will or ability to get back up. You have something to offer in everyone's life—from a smile, to a hug, to a hand up. Your attitude and actions bless people richly and can cause people to get up and get back on the road to success.

> Lord, I want to give generously, even financially,
> knowing you multiply my gifts with your abundance. Amen.

Him-Possible

"For nothing will be impossible with God."
–LUKE 1:37 ESV

We have been called to not doubt, but to believe God in addition to believing in God. Most, if not all of us, have a story in our lives where something wonderful–even miraculous–happened and we have no explanation for it except God. All of us have been challenged with circumstances completely out of our control, when all we could do was trust God and His decision for us.

Just in case you haven't been told, *nothing* is impossible with God. Anything that is in the will of God is possible with Him. What does that mean to you? Think about something in your life that you've held on to because you thought it was impossible to do or solve. A dream? A problem? An addiction that needed breaking? A disease that needed healing? A marriage or child that needed restoring? Finances, relationships, students, desires of your heart? What have you marked off as impossible? If there is something you believe you can't do, know that you're standing at the threshold of a miracle.

Lord, I believe nothing is impossible with you.
Amen.

Determined Days

A person's days are determined; you have decreed the
number of his months and have set limits he cannot exceed.
–Job 14:5 NIV

For many Christians, witnessing to an unsaved friend, neighbor,
or loved one is one of the most frightening tasks they could
ever do. When asked to love and forgive an enemy, it seems impossible. To turn the other cheek comes with an expectancy of
the sting of the next slap. The challenge to seek God with *all*
of our heart, soul, mind, and strength seems unattainable when
our heart is burdened, our mind is slipping, and our strength is
zapped.

Today I want to remind you that our days have been determined; our time is short. We don't know the number of our days,
or of anyone else's. We don't know when we'll run out of time to
forgive, love, apologize, encourage, or testify to the love of God
to those who don't know Jesus died for them. Don't let fear or
fatigue slow you down. The clock is ticking, make the most of
every moment.

Lord, thank you for life. I am determined
to meet and complete your challenge. Amen.

Humble Harmony

Finally, all of you, be likeminded, be sympathetic,
love as brothers, be compassionate and humble.
Do not repay evil with evil or insult with insult, but with
blessing, because to this you were called so that you
may inherit a blessing. –1 PETER 3:8–9 NIV

What hinders harmony? Living harmoniously in our relationships—whether with family, spouse, students, friends, or even
your enemies—means we must love, serve, sacrifice for, and forgive *before* we are asked. Love does not keep score. We cannot
expect anything from others in return, have a hidden agenda, or
seek revenge.

It is not easy to live in harmony; it takes a humble spirit and
self-control. It means looking at others' needs before our own. It
means saying, "I'm sorry," first. It takes prayer and remembering
Christ's sacrifice and love on the cross. We are a blessing because
we are blessed in Christ.

If you have a relationship in discord, ask yourself—better yet,
ask the other person—how you could better love and serve them.
If they have hurt you in any way, forgive them as your Father in
heaven has forgiven you.

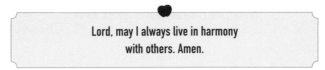

Lord, may I always live in harmony
with others. Amen.

Go through It

Even though I walk through the valley of the shadow of death, I fear no evil, for You are with me; Your rod and Your staff, they comfort me. –PSALM 23:4

There's a children's song called "Going on a Bear Hunt." A hunter encounters several obstacles while hunting a bear; he comes upon a cornfield, a tree, a river, and a cave. At each obstacle, the hunter sings that he can't go over it or around it, so he'll have to go through it. Remember that song?

We are journeying through life, hunting for something, and we hit obstacles—obstacles that we can't go over or around. We have to go through them. Think of some past obstacles. Did you look for a way around, calculate your next steps, or question your goal? Perhaps you turned and ran all the way home, like the hunter. Which response was most rewarding? Which one was most difficult? And what lessons did you learn?

Know that you never face your obstacles alone; Jesus is with you. Let Him be your courage through current and future obstacles.

Jesus, you sustain me in everything
I go through. Amen.

Created to Give Glory

"You are worthy, our Lord and God, to receive glory
and honor and power, for you created all things,
and by your will they were created and have their being."
—REVELATION 4:11 NIV

While sharing Jesus with some young people in my town, I met "Daniel." Daniel believed that he was created by his parents, not God. He believed that he was born with no purpose and no destiny, and that through his own strength and wisdom he would add to humanity and be remembered for his deeds. How scary and burdensome to think it is all up you.

Imagine what it would feel like to believe that you had to plan and arrange all you accomplished, using your own resources that you had to obtain on your own. Imagine working alone every day for a place in the world's hall of fame. Chances are good that you have students and coworkers who think this way. How do they get through the hard times and push past failure? Now consider how knowing God is in control makes our lives different. We are Christ's blessed creation. Give Him glory and honor as His cherished creation.

> Lord, may I rejoice as God's creation
> and rest in His power. Amen.

Guarded and Guided

Your word is a lamp to my feet and a light to my path.
—Psalm 119:105

Oswald Chambers writes, "The great enemy of the life of faith in God is not sin, but the good which is not good enough. The good is always the enemy of the best."* God's Word is essential to our sustainability, success, and ability to discern good from God's best.

When we trade *great* for *good*, it tempts us off the path where God's Word guides and provides. It steals our attention, kills our effectiveness, and destroys our destiny as the enemy steers us off course in a cleverly disguised plot of "good" that is not at all what God had in mind for us. In some cases, we miss His plan in doubt or fear, or steal someone else's blessing as we swoop in to take a task we can easily accomplish but was planned to grow someone else. We guard against this with courageous prayer and times of listening and obeying God; He will guide and guard us to reach and accomplish His best.

> Jesus, guard and guide me to and
> through your best path. Amen.

---

* Oswald Chambers, "The Good or the Best?" *My Utmost for His Highest,* accessed February 28, 2017, https://webcache.googleusercontent.com/search?q=cache:
Vn88sqsjNUUJ:https://utmost.org/the-good-or-the-best/+&cd=1&hl=en&ct=
clnk&gl=us.

Introductions and Invitations

How then will they call on him in whom they have not believed? And how are they to believe in him of whom they have never heard? And how are they to hear without someone preaching? —ROMANS 10:14 ESV

It can be difficult to understand how someone, especially someone living in America, could not have heard of Jesus. Even so, there are thousands, if not millions, of people who don't know Him. They may have heard His name, but they don't know any truth about Him. Millions don't know His attributes, His promises, or His ways; they have no idea that He has a loving, wonderful plan for their life. Grace and mercy are mysteries to them.

Have you assumed that everyone in your town, school, and country has been introduced to Jesus? God has given you the assignment to share His love and message. Invite people to learn the facts about the one true, everlasting, loving Savior, so that they might hear and believe.

> Lord, help me to introduce people to you
> and invite them to grow in their faith in you. Amen.

I Can Sympathize

For we do not have a high priest who cannot sympathize
with our weaknesses, but One who has been tempted in
all things as we are, yet without sin. —Hebrews 4:15

I was excited to earn my master's degree in seminary, but it was a lot of hard work and long hours. I wanted to be a good example to my children who saw me get up early and stay up late. They watched me work through the weekend and say no to many social invitations. I wanted them to realize the value of the education and the discipline that it takes to be successful. Neither of my children will ever be able to say to me, "You don't know how hard it is!" I did it first, and they know it wasn't easy. They also know they can come to me for sympathy because I have experienced how difficult college can be.

This journey has made me think of Jesus' earthly life. Sometimes I forget that He was "tempted in all things"; satan tempted and toiled trying to stop Him. We can never say to Him, "You don't know _____."

Jesus, thank you for your sympathy
and strength in my weakness. Amen.

Know, Flow, and Go

"Be appalled," … declares the LORD. "For My people have committed two evils: They have forsaken Me, the fountain of living waters, to hew for themselves cisterns, broken cisterns that can hold no water." –JEREMIAH 2:12–13

God spoke in the Old and New Testaments about His abundant provision–living water, which not only sustains us but revives and renews us as we rely on Him. The problem is that His people continued to rely on the things, people, and false gods of this world. Instead of letting the blessings of God flow through them, they built up a dam in their hearts and minds, trying to keep a reservoir filled only for themselves. The result, according to God, was stinky, spoiled life that was empty and unsatisfying.

We are blessed to be a blessing, comforted to comfort others, and given opportunities to share, not to stockpile. An educator's life is far from a life of leisure, but everyone has something to offer–time, talent, and treasure. Who do you know that could use a cup of kindness?

Lord, let living water flow through me
like a rushing river. Amen.

Love Letters

And he gave to Moses, when he had finished speaking with him on Mount Sinai, the two tablets of the testimony, tablets of stone, written with the finger of God. –Exodus 31:18 esv

When was the last time you received a handwritten letter? It is such a personal expression of thoughtfulness to put words on paper that convey what our heart is feeling and our mind is thinking. We send cards to show compassion, give comfort or congratulations, offer thanks, and celebrate an occasion. In the modern world of Snapchat and Twitter, lengthy letters are a thing of the past, so encourage or even assign your students to write you a letter. Determine the subject or let them choose it; either way, it will help them practice a skill they will need throughout life.

God wrote us a long love letter–the Bible. It is filled with information and inspiration to encourage and equip us for life. He even wrote the Ten Commandments with His own hand–His mind and heart written in stone for us!

> Lord, may I be intentional about reading your love letter to me. Amen.

Hard Heads, Hard Hearts, and Hard Times

But they did not obey nor incline their ear, but made their neck stiff, that they might not hear nor receive instruction.
–JEREMIAH 17:23 NKJV

How do you react to instruction? Do you receive it well or do you rebel? Have you ever said, "I don't like being told what to do"? If you have, you're not alone. The Israelites had this problem too; they wanted to be blessed but not bossed.

What gets in the way of our obedience? Could it be that it's our own hard heads? Sometimes we're so stubborn that we believe that we know all the answers, we're in control, or that things could never be any other way but our way. Consider how well your students learn if they refuse to listen.

Or is it a hard heart that gets in the way of our obedience? Has something from your past, such as a hurt or disappointment, caused you to walk away from God instead of toward Him? Or perhaps you're pushing Him away instead of drawing nearer? Keep in mind that hard heads and hard hearts lead to hard time s.

Lord, guard my heart and guide my head
for your—and my—benefit. Amen.

Magnify

O magnify the LORD with me, and let us
exalt His name together. –PSALM 34:3

When you think of magnifying something, you think of increasing its size, but we all know that God is unlimited, so we can't actually increase Him. However, we can expand His presence in our mind, heart, and community by magnifying Him with our lips and lives, which means we proclaim His greatness and exalt Him as we live and love through His power.

Focusing on God's greatness and His blessings will cause our affection, our awareness, and our appreciation for Him to grow. We expand His impact in our lives when we submit to His authority, and we increase as educators as we invite Him into our schools and seek His wisdom to teach and live. As a result, we proclaim what He has done for us and through us, and we exalt Him in our school, our community, and all the earth.

We magnify Christ alone. If we magnify our problems, they block our view of God's solutions. If we magnify ourselves or other people, it blocks our minds from His wisdom and blocks our lives from His blessings. Open your lips to exalt Him and open your life to His love.

> Lord, may I magnify you and you alone,
> and may I exalt you with other believers. Amen.

God Is Your Praise

He is your praise; He is your God, who performed
for you those great and awesome wonders you saw
with your own eyes. –DEUTERONOMY 10:21

I have heard it said that if we enter God's gates with thanksgiving and His courts with praise then complaining must be the praise music of hell. Of course, everyone complains at times, but we have to be intentional about preventing it from being our first language.

Sometimes, if satan cannot change our actions, he works against our attitudes. We go to church but find everything wrong with how it is done. We go to work but tell everyone how we'd rather be home. This way of speaking and living satisfies satan because it ignores the good things God does in our lives. While we might not understand what the Lord is doing in our current season, we can always look back to His faithfulness in the past.

Our lives are a living testimony that will praise someone—either God or satan. Choose wisely.

Lord, thank you for the opportunity, this week
and always, to live a testimony of your praise. Amen.

Stirring

And let us consider how to stir up one another
to love and good works. –HEBREWS 10:24 ESV

What does an encouraging word mean to you? Think about what stirs you to do something great–to go the extra mile or push through when you're exhausted or frustrated. Perhaps it's respect or appreciation, or a heartening, "You can do it!" Or maybe it's the inspiration you feel when someone is willing to come alongside you and walk with you through a season of decision, responsibility, or challenge.

Who do you turn to when you need encouragement? Do you have a "positive partner," a fellow educator or best friend who you can count on for prayer and a smile? Make it a point to be encouraging, stirring people on to what is good and right in the eyes of the Lord. Steer clear of people who like to "stir the pot" or "stir up trouble." Earn a reputation for being a light–a positive encourager who charges people up to overcome and overachieve.

> Jesus, you are my greatest encourager. Stir me,
> and help me to stir others, to love and good deeds. Amen.

Satan the Enemy

Be alert and of sober mind. Your enemy the devil prowls around like a roaring lion looking for someone to devour.
—1 PETER 5:8 NIV

B rayden, Connor, and Tyler wanted to play baseball. Brayden's mom said they could play down the street but not in the backyard because of the proximity to the neighbors. Brayden obeyed this rule, but the other two did not; they had buddied up with Brayden because of his great backyard and hitting ability. Connor and Tyler chipped away at Brayden's resolve, and promising to be careful and quiet, they snuck to the backyard. A few minutes later, a baseball broke a window, and Connor and Tyler left Brayden alone to take the blame and punishment.

Have you ever had a friend, or even a work team, urge you to "bend" the rules only to leave you standing alone when things turned sour? Satan tempts us to take the easy way, to justify our desires or think that God's rules don't apply to us. Then when disaster strikes, he laughs and leaves. As today's Scripture says, he is looking to devour. He wants to kill, steal, and destroy, so be on your guard.

Lord, keep me alert against satan's schemes.
Amen.

Shielded

My God, my rock, in whom I take refuge, my shield and
the horn of my salvation, my stronghold and my refuge;
my savior, You save me from violence. –2 SAMUEL 22:3

Viruses are constantly being sent throughout the Internet, and we need to be careful not to download them onto our computer. One summer our school district's computers had to be left on because a virus was in its e-mail system. (A virus uses the boot time to hack into the systems and tell the computer to do something different from what it's programmed to do.) The shield that the IT workers installed finally detected and removed the virus so that the computers could run normally again.

Satan tries to hack into our lives and reprogram us to sin. The Holy Spirit is the shield that God has installed in us to detect and defeat satan's viruses. Think about what kind of tools satan is using to try to hack into your students' lives. Video games, movies, insecurity, and ungodly friends are some of his favorite viruses. Pray that God would shield you and your students.

Lord, may I not let satan's viruses tell me
to do something different from what you have
designed me to do. Amen.

Rhema

And the tempter came and said to Him, "If You are
the Son of God, command that these stones become bread."
But He answered and said, "It is written, 'Man shall not
live on bread alone, but on every word that proceeds
out of the mouth of God.'" –MATTHEW 4:3–4

God loves to talk with His children. We ask Him to give wisdom and guidance—a *rhema* (or utterance) to show us His will. In the verse above, Jesus, quoting Deuteronomy 8:3, professes that life comes from *rhema*; God speaks and supplies all our needs. *Rhema* moves us from being rooted in routine to rooted in Christ. Always wait on the prompting and clarity from God's mouth that you need to proceed.

Take time today to be with God and to listen for fresh *rhema*. The Holy Spirit will fill every space that you yield to Him. Profess your desire for His kingdom come and His will be done in your life as it is in heaven.

Lord, my ears and heart listen to
receive your rhema. Amen.

Concert of Glory

May the God of endurance and encouragement grant
you to live in such harmony with one another, in accord
with Christ Jesus, that together you may with one voice
glorify the God and Father of our Lord Jesus Christ.
–ROMANS 15:5–6 ESV

We have been abundantly blessed with life, love, and opportunity; we have been given friends, family, and a host of acquaintances that touch our lives in big and small ways. God gives us encouragement and endurance to have patience, stamina, and success in all circumstances and relationships.

One of the greatest gifts He has given us is "togetherness"; He has given us relationships with other Christ-followers to walk, work, and worship in unity. Unity within the body of Christ is like a concert of praise to Jesus, and a concert of glory to Him for the world to see and hear. The harmony of our lives and voices lifted up under the love and authority of Jesus is a beautiful instrument of His glory, and draws others to want to join us.

> Lord, let the way I love and live be in harmony with
> your followers and always to your glory. Amen.

Scattered by Self–Sufficiency

They said, "Come, let us build for ourselves a city, and a
tower whose top will reach into heaven, and let us make
for ourselves a name, otherwise we will be scattered abroad
over the face of the whole earth." –GENESIS 11:4

It is vital to set our mind and motives on God's will and ways.
When we as God's people let self-sufficiency creep in, it begins to
dominate our attitudes and actions. God had not given His people
a spirit of unity to build a city for themselves, but rather so they
could participate in building a kingdom for God. Instead of bow-
ing to the blessing of heaven reaching down to touch them, they
began believing and building a way for earth to touch heaven.

The power of unity, which was unstoppable in obedience to
God's will, came to a screeching halt when man put his own desires above God. The only way up is to bow down and humble
ourselves. God came down, and Babel became a town of useless
chatter, shattered and scattered. Submit yourself to God's will,
and He will make you succeed.

Lord, I desire for my life to be built
on you and for you. Amen.

His Helpful Example

"For I gave you an example that you also should do as I did to you. Truly, truly, I say to you, a slave is not greater than his master, nor is one who is sent greater than the one who sent him. If you know these things, you are blessed if you do them." –JOHN 13:15–17

Jesus expects us to know and follow the example He set for us. Think about the love He gave, the patience He had, the teachings He offered, and especially the sacrifice He made for all of us. He who knew no sin took our punishment so we could know Him and grow in His example until we "graduate" to heaven.

He knows your struggles and your pain. He knows what it is like to have friends, to laugh and share, and to have them betray you. He knows what it feels like to be exhausted, rejected, tempted, and beaten. He also knows what it feels like to be loved, appreciated, welcomed, and exalted. He certainly knows what it is like to be a teacher!

What examples are you especially grateful for from Christ's earthly life?

Jesus, thank you for your example.
Bless me as I follow you. Amen.

Proof of Faith

> In this you greatly rejoice, even though now for a little
> while, if necessary, you have been distressed by various
> trials, so that the proof of your faith, being more precious
> than gold … may be found to result in praise and glory and
> honor at the revelation of Jesus Christ. –1 Peter 1:6–7

How do we prove our faith? We express our love for Christ through worship, prayer, mission work, and so on, but how do we express faith? Our greatest expressions of faith come in our trials.

If asked, "Do you have faith?" I'm sure you would respond, "Definitely!" Uncertainty allows us the opportunity to live out what we say we believe. Trials in our school or marriage, illnesses, and issues with our students or children, aging parents, or finances bring us to our knees to say, "Lord, I know you have this under control, so I rest in your love and wisdom."

We don't need to know what will happen tomorrow or how things will turn out–not what, when, why, or how. We just need to know Jesus.

> Lord, may I always remember that you love me
> more than I can understand and that you have things
> all under control. I just need to trust you. Amen.

Watching for Jesus, Part 1

> Immediately he made his disciples get into the boat
> and go before him to the other side, to Bethsaida,
> while he dismissed the crowd. And … he went up on the
> mountain to pray. … And he saw that they were making
> headway painfully, for the wind was against them.
> And about the fourth watch of the night he came to them,
> walking on the sea. —MARK 6:45–48 ESV

This story is found in three of the Gospels, each with a different emphasis. Matthew and Mark tell that Jesus had "made" His disciples board the boat. Somehow, I bet some resisted because the Greek word for *made* is *anagkazo*, which means by force. I picture Peter's resistance, wanting to stay with Jesus and not wanting to miss a moment or miracle. But Jesus had bigger plans.

Realize that Jesus knows your storms are coming, and sometimes He places you in them. He sees you and has something great for you. Jesus is miles away praying when He "sees them straining at the oars." He sees us even when we don't see Him, and He will never leave us.

> Jesus, may I always watch for you
> in the storms. Amen.

Watching for Jesus, Part 2

And about the fourth watch of the night he came
to them, walking on the sea. He meant to pass by them.
—MARK 6:48 ESV

Perhaps you're wondering what it means that Jesus "meant to pass by them." It almost sounds like He was going to race them across the sea or leave them there to struggle.

When Moses asked to see God in Exodus 33:18–23, God told him, "You cannot see my face," but then went on to say, "While My glory is passing by, I will … cover you … until I have passed by." Likewise, Jesus was showing the disciples that He was not just a good man or great prophet; He was (and still is) God!

Mark points us to understand that, in Old Testament terminology, Jesus' intention was to reveal His glory to His disciples. He meant to pass by them so they would recognize Him as Messiah. Jesus steps into the boat, and for the first time in the Gospels, Matthew 14:32 records that they worshiped Him. They recognized and responded to His glory! May we always do the same.

Jesus, you are God! I am in awe of you.
and I worship you on the waves of life. Amen.

Desperate Days to Desired Haven

Then they cried to the LORD in their trouble,
and He brought them out of their distresses. He caused the
storm to be still, so that the waves of the sea were hushed.
Then they were glad because they were quiet, so He guided
them to their desired haven. –PSALM 107:28–30

The people of our nation have found themselves in trouble in several areas, including being deep in debt. So what are we to do? We must humble ourselves and ask God to help us to prioritize Him and His will to be good stewards of His resources. Debt makes us a slave to the ones we owe and the stuff we do not really own.

As a part of the church, we must make the first move. It is not the job of the government to change or save us. We must cry out to the Lord so that He stills the storm and leads us to our safe haven where we can follow Him to financial and spiritual peace.

What changes do you need to make personally? Just imagine what this world would look like if every Christian obeyed God in everything He has said.

Lord, I want to walk in your ways. Please lead the way
for our nation to reach your desired destination. Amen.

Praying in His Presence

You scrutinize my path and my lying down, and are
intimately acquainted with all my ways. Even before there
is a word on my tongue, behold, O LORD, You know it all.
—PSALM 139:3–4

Learning to increase our prayer life begins by realizing that God made us, knows us, loves us, and is always with us. It becomes our delight to practice living in His presence. Just as we would carry on a conversation with someone walking or working with us throughout the day, our prayers can become a conversation with God that goes far beyond our quiet time.

We can praise Him when we see something beautiful in creation, and thank Him every time we receive His favor, blessing, or help. We can say short sentences or carry on long conversations as we commute, exercise, or mow the lawn. He reads our thoughts and hearts, and that mind-set helps prayer become a lifestyle of living with Him, through Him, and for Him.

> Lord, I lift up my prayers—my thoughts, thanks,
> concerns, and confessions—as I remember that
> I am always in your presence. Amen.

Practicing His Presence

Where can I go from Your Spirit? Or where can I flee from
Your presence? If I ascend to heaven … [or] if I dwell in the
remotest part of the sea, even there Your hand will lead me.
—PSALM 139:7–10

Living in the loving awareness of God's constant presence is a
passion, comfort, and assurance of love, provision, protection,
and security. It gives us pause to pray through our days and consider His ways in respect and response to our relationship with
Him. It also gives God an open invitation to release His generous
blessings on our life.

Practicing His presence includes considering His calling before we commit, and praying through triumphs and trials. It is
a life that learns what it means to have the Holy Spirit prompt
us, recognizing the feeling we get when we know something is
wrong and we shouldn't do it. It is hearing the voice inside that
tells us to call and check on someone, to go somewhere, or to
do something. It is the peace and comfort we experience when
circumstances should have us in chaos.

Lord, let my life be the glorifying product
of practicing your presence. Amen.

Prayerful

Always be joyful. Never stop praying.
—1 THESSALONIANS 5: 16–17 NLT

There is no substitute for prayer. We need time alone talking with and listening to our heavenly Father, and we need times of corporate prayer, praying with other followers of Jesus. Good communication with Jesus is even more important in our relationship with Him than it is in our earthly relationships. We would never think to not talk with our spouse, family, or close friends all day. God wants to talk with us throughout our day, as we come and go, through various emotions and experiences and when we need help or are prompted to say thank you.

Be aware of His unceasing presence and cognizant that every word or thought is part of an ongoing conversation with Him. Praise Him, call out for help, thank Him, and talk to Him about the people and places around you. Bless His handiwork and beauty in creation, and express your trust in Him. You don't need to be eloquent or elaborate; just speak from your heart.

Lord, thank you for always walking and talking
with me throughout my life. Amen.

July

At an Acceptable Time

My prayer is to You, O LORD, at an acceptable time;
O God, in the greatness of Your lovingkindness,
answer me with Your saving truth. May the flood of
water not overflow me nor the deep swallow me up,
nor the pit shut its mouth on me. –PSALM 69:13, 15

In our prayers, sometimes we wait patiently on Him; we let go of some things easier than others when the answer seems to be no. Then there are times of tragedy when we cry out and waiting is excruciating.

Have you ever felt like this Scripture describes, sinking in deep waters or in a pit that is closing? All of us have probably gone through a tragedy when we were on our knees begging God to answer us *quickly*. We may even find ourselves pleading with Jesus to answer exactly as we want.

God always answers our prayers, and He does so in His best time and out of His goodness and love for us—even if it doesn't feel like it at the time.

Lord, may I have faith in the pain
and in the gain. Amen.

Where His Glory Dwells

O LORD, I love the habitation of Your house and
the place where Your glory dwells. —PSALM 26:8

The Jewish people had a deep love for the house of God, the Jewish Temple. It is most often called the house; it is where God sent His presence and glory to dwell.

Through the Holy Spirit, we are walking, worshipping houses of His glory. Jesus never leaves us, and 100 percent of our life is spent in worship of Him, whether we realize it or not. Every minute at work, recreation, time with your friends and family, house and yardwork, prayer, Bible study, and every other activity is an act of living out your love and purpose in Him and for Him.

God has placed you in a family, neighborhood, school, church, and so on to love people with His love and accomplish His purposes for this time in this place. The Spirit is sealed in you. Therefore everything you do every day blesses your earthly country and God's kingdom. His glory dwells in you and *all* you do.

> Jesus, every day, every affection and action
> of my life shows and shares my love for you.

Diligent

The soul of the sluggard craves and gets nothing, while the soul of the diligent is richly supplied. –Proverbs 13:4 ESV

Do you have a bucket list? Our family had one long before the movie premiered. The idea is to make a list of things—personal, spiritual, professional, and relational—that you would like to do before you die (or "kick the bucket"). The list should include places you would like to go, things you would like to see, adventurous and academic feats, and perhaps even a purchase or two. It may include seeing a Broadway show in New York or visiting the Holy Land. It may include getting your master's degree or sending your child to college without incurring the debt of student loans. You may want to write a book or read through the Bible.

A bucket list helps us not only to dream, but also set goals and live life deliberately. Dreams and goals allow us to plan, save, prepare, and work toward something special in the amazing world God has created.

> Lord, thank you for this amazing world.
> I will work diligently to make the
> most of every opportunity. Amen.

God Bless America

May God be merciful and bless us. May his face
smile with favor on us. —PSALM 67:1 NLT

Irving Berlin was a Jewish immigrant who moved to New York
from Russia in 1893. He wrote over fifteen hundred songs,
many for Broadway and film. You probably know, or at least
recognize, dozens of his songs, but the one we sing most often is
"God Bless America."

Berlin began writing this song in 1918 when he was serving
in the United States Army. He later revised some of the lyrics,
before it was introduced to the nation in November of 1938, to
clarify it as a prayer and not a political song. In fact, it has an in-
troductory verse (that few people know) that states it is a prayer.

We have become accustomed to the song simply beginning
with "God bless America." The next time you sing this song,
whether at school or elsewhere, remember that you are lifting a
prayer to God.

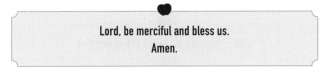

Lord, be merciful and bless us.
Amen.

Appointment with God

Do you not know? Have you not heard? The Everlasting God, the LORD, the Creator of the ends of the earth does not become weary or tired. His understanding is inscrutable. He gives strength to the weary, and to him who lacks might He increases power. —ISAIAH 40:28–29

Have you ever needed to make an appointment with someone, only to find that it will be weeks or even months until they will see you? It might be that they're too busy, not interested in your situation, or don't want to get involved.

It is important that you talk to the right authority—the One who can help and wants to do so whenever you need it, without an appointment He will listen anytime, anywhere, and is always interested in and concerned for you. He wants to be deeply involved in your life, and has all the facts. He is wise and just. He knows the solution and the path to get you there. The one true Expert on all matters is always available to you. In fact, He would love to hear from you right now.

Lord, prompt me to always talk to you first.
Amen.

Don't Miss the Way

Desire without knowledge is not good—how much more
will hasty feet miss the way. —Proverbs 19:2 NIV

Vacations at the beach can take us from a cheetah's sprint to a snail's crawl.

Once when some friends were visiting us, we grabbed our buckets and headed up the beach to Sand Dollar Island. They chose an aerobic pace while I took in the sights and shells along the way. When I finally arrived at the island, I couldn't find my friends anywhere; they'd walked right by the island that was covered with people searching for sand dollars. They not only missed the destination but a bucket full of shells and memories.

Can your life get so crazy that you get caught up just getting through and getting to? Do you ever say, "We just have to get through … (conferences, winter recess, training, the pre-Christmas break crazies, testing, budget, staffing, and so on)," and before you know it, you're wondering where the year went? Take care not to miss the "shoreline" of blessings along the way.

> Lord, teach me to enjoy the journey of the rest of
> this year and life. I don't want to miss your gifts. Amen.

Building Up

Let no corrupting talk come out of your mouths, but only such as is good for building up, as fits the occasion, that it may give grace to those who hear. —Ephesians 4:29 ESV

Have you ever heard the saying, "Loose lips sink ships"? Your words hold amazing power. They can build up people to teach, give confidence, and encourage, and stir others on to glorious achievements. Your students, family, and friends can give many testimonies of how your words gave them the strength, wisdom, or inspiration they needed to take on greater feats. You will be quoted and noted throughout the lives of many people. Just listen to other people talk about advice or encouragement they've been given. They say things like, "My mama always said …" or "As my second-grade teacher used to say …"

Words are sticky. They have a way of clinging to our hearts and minds, and even giving us wings when life tries to weigh us down. What will you be quoted as saying?

Lord, let my words always build up.
Keep my tongue from tearing down. Amen.

Friend

And the scripture was fulfilled that says,
"Abraham believed God, and it was credited to
him as righteousness," and he was called God's friend.
–JAMES 2:23 NIV

Three girls at the pool agreed to go under the water together. They held hands and counted, "One, two, three," ... and they *all* stopped. None of them intended on going under, but they each went through the motions up until the time to take the plunge. They were shocked and mad. None of them followed through, so what kind of friends were they?

Can you think of a time when a "friend" gave their word and then broke it? Have you ever had an all-for-one-and-one-for-all pact with a group only to have them run for the hills when the going got tough? How comforting it is to know that Jesus is our true-blue, all-the-way-to-the-cross-for-you friend! He always keeps His Word.

Think about what characteristics are important to you in a friendship. Is there a trait you would like to improve in yourself as a friend? Has anyone ever taken the plunge with you in a tough situation? If so, thank God for their loyalty and then emulate it in your friendships.

Lord, may I be a true friend to others.
Amen.

Insulated or Isolated

He will cover you with his pinions, and under his wings
you will find refuge; his faithfulness is a shield and buckler.
—PSALM 91:4 ESV

Satan loves for us to isolate ourselves so he can lie to us and
fan the fires of our hurts, doubts, and pity parties. God wants
to insulate us during quiet times alone for rest, relaxation, read-
ing/studying, and praying, but He also calls us to relationships.
When we avoid being with people because we are angry, hurt,
or embarrassed, we open the door that the enemy likes to slip in
through to talk to us.

You know the voice. It makes you feel angry or paralyzed,
and it makes you feel ashamed, stupid, or superior. The voice
isolates you further, making you push away people who are trying to show you love. When ice is insulated, it is sustained and
performs its purpose; when removed from insulation, it quickly
loses its form and function. Satan calls you away from Christ's
covering, so evaluate your life. Are you isolated or insulated?
Seek cover in Christ.

> Lord, I seek refuge under your wings.
> Insulate me so that I may be shielded and
> sustained for your kingdom. Amen.

Brokenhearted

For You do not delight in sacrifice, otherwise I would
give it. … The sacrifices of God are a broken spirit;
a broken and a contrite heart, O God, You will not despise.
—PSALM 51:16–17

Today's verses were written by David as he faced God with a guilty heart. His heart and life were full of sin. David and Nathan the prophet knew it, and, worst of all, God knew it. David recognized that sacrifices would not appease God; He wanted David's heart instead. David would have to repent and hand his heart to God for restoration.

The Hebrew word for *contrite* is *dakah*, which means to crush to pieces. Coupled with the word *broken*, it means to shatter and crush. God wants us to be brokenhearted over our sin.

Ask Him to reveal if you become hardened by sin. If you have, repent and ask God to crush your heart so He can repair and restore it. A whole heart is only made possible by God, who will not let sin come between you and Him. Sounds like true love!

> Lord, I bring my broken heart to you,
> emptied of sin and ready to be filled with you. Amen.

Still

Be still, and know that I am God!
—Psalm 46:10 NLT

When was the last time you were still? I mean really still—mind and body, not thinking about what you needed to do or pondering the past or future but settling your whole body down and being still. Take a moment—and a deep breath—and be still. Focus your thoughts on God, and picture sitting in His presence in a calm, tranquil place and being flooded with peace in the presence of His power and love.

You may be in a busy season of life, or maybe you just think that life is supposed to be filled with constant movement and that the demands on your life are "normal." Be still and ask God if you have taken on anything that He did not will for your life. Did you say yes when He wanted you to say no? Maybe you are asking Him for answers; if so, be still and listen. You cannot fill up a moving car; you have to stop and shut the motor off. Be still and be filled.

Lord, you are God and I am not.
Fill me as I am still in your presence. Amen.

Restored

Restore to me the joy of your salvation,
and make me willing to obey you. —PSALM 51:12 NLT

The offer of salvation is an offer of victory. Jesus paid the ultimate price as our sacrifice, so that we could be saved from the eternal consequences of our sin. God created us, continuously guides us, and disciples us toward our purpose. Jesus' life, death, and resurrection was much more than a rescue mission; it was a restoration mission. He paid restitution for our sin and re-established the relationship necessary in order to fully live life. We now have abundant life as He trains us, teaches us, and tests us so that we can fulfill our earthly destiny and receive our eternal reward.

We wake up every morning with choices—be lazy or diligent, move forward or backward, rise up or sink deeper, or choose success or despair. Pray for people who choose the path of fools at the crossroads of taking the path to success or the road of distraction and disobedience. How can we help them realize their need, repent of their sin, re-engage with their destiny, be rescued from wrath, and receive their reward?

Lord, help me to fully realize the joy and
reward you have restored. Amen.

Labeled "In Christ"

I have been crucified with Christ. It is no longer I who live,
but Christ who lives in me. —GALATIANS 2:20 ESV

One hot summer afternoon, two high school boys came to my
front door taking a poll and handing out materials for the political party of their choice. They were entering their senior year,
and were spending their summer serving in a variety of volunteer
and internship positions because they were interested in politics
and concerned for our nation. The boys were polite and well-spo-
ken, with college plans in politics and engineering, and while both
were student leaders at school, they labeled themselves "nerds."

I asked myself why. Was it because they were active in their
community, forward-thinkers, or concerned citizens taking action
to make a change? Was it because they'd set future goals and
were working to reach them instead of spending the summer at
the pool? Maybe they considered "nerd" the label of leadership
and responsibility.

How would you label them? As they left, I prayed that they
would label themselves in the love and leading of Jesus.

Lord, I label myself "in Christ," living in
the love and leadership of you. Amen.

Power of Prayer

The LORD is far from the wicked, but he hears
the prayer of the righteous. —PROVERBS 15:29 NIV

What is prayer? Why do you pray? And what are the results of prayer? Take some time to really think about your answers.

Prayer is focused, often sustained, attention and time with God. It is a personal conversation expressing many feelings, events in life, and intercession for others. Prayer is an opportunity to grow our relationship with God; to show love, trust, and praise to Him; and to express our need for Him.

We pray to grow closer to God, because it delights Him and He desires to hear our prayers—whether they are in desperation or to express joy and thanks. Prayer releases emotion and our circumstances into God's hands. It puts things and life in perspective with God's love and power.

Here are some of the results of prayer: renewal, refreshment, receiving of God's answers or blessing, reassurance, rest, revealing of God's plan, reward, refocusing, redirecting of our path and attention, reconciliation through confession of sin, and relationship grown and nurtured.

Lord, thank you for hearing
and answering my prayers. Amen.

Our Identity in His Love

Be strengthened with power through His Spirit in the
inner man, so that Christ may dwell in your hearts
through faith; and that you, being rooted and grounded in
love, may be able to comprehend with all the saints what is
the breadth and length and height and depth, and to know
the love of Christ which surpasses knowledge, that you may
be filled up to all the fullness of God. –EPHESIANS 3:16–19

Christ alone gives us our worth, and His love for us is all we
need to know that we are not just "somebody" but "somebody
special," loved from the beginning of time. Our identity is in Him,
not in a person, position, or possession. His loving thoughts toward us are more than the grains of sand on a beach, and His
love will never fail or leave us. It is the only love that is truly
always and forever.

We need earthly relationships. No one wants to be alone or
ignored, but we can never compromise God's place, plans, or
commands so someone can be in our life.

> Lord, may I find and define love,
> fulfillment, and purpose in Christ. Amen.

The Great Compromise

Happy are those who obey his decrees and search for him with all their hearts. *They do not compromise with evil, and they walk only in his paths.* —PSALM 119:2–3 NLT

In 1787, delegates met to create the government structure of our new country. It was a daunting task with a canyon of disagreement that needed to be bridged. A solution came in the Connecticut Compromise, or the Great Compromise, which met the needs and bridged the gap between both sides. Compromise is to meet halfway, to give and take, and to bargain or deal. A real compromise meets the needs without either party losing the core of what they value most.

Have you ever been asked to compromise, but it required you to sin? God's commands are not up for discussion; He does not compromise. What do you think of when you hear the word *tolerance*? Have you ever been asked or instructed to compromise your beliefs and values at school? If so, how did you react, and do you have any regrets?

We don't compromise to be happy; Scripture says that happiness is a result of obeying God's decrees.

Lord, give me wisdom to know when
I should and shouldn't compromise. Amen.

"B" a Blessing

Because of the service by which you have proved
yourselves, men will praise God for the obedience
that accompanies your confession of the gospel of Christ,
and for your generosity in sharing with them
and with everyone else. −2 CORINTHIANS 9:13 NIV

We are *blessed* to be a blessing. God blesses us with talents, money, time, wisdom, and other resources so we can turn around and bless others with them.

We might not think of suffering as a blessing, but good, glory to God, and ministry can come from the experience gained through pain. Trials and struggles cause us to *bend* but not break; we are called to a higher response that reflects our faith. We must *believe* to be a blessing.

We would all love to be *blessed* to be a blessing. Given the chance to choose, we would probably all choose *blessed* instead of the chance to *bend* or *believe* in adversity. God gives us all three opportunities to grow and glorify. Think about times in your life when you were blessed, bent, or called to believe? How were you ultimately blessed in the end?

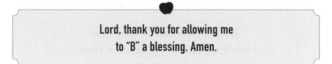

Lord, thank you for allowing me
to "B" a blessing. Amen.

Perfect

You therefore must be perfect,
as your heavenly Father is perfect. —Matthew 5:48 esv

After reading that verse, you might think, *You have to be kidding me!* We all know only one perfect man walked this earth, and it was not you or me. How then can we be perfect?

Matthew 5 is Jesus' lesson on being blessed and set apart—happy and holy, in the original Hebrew definitions. It's a life that causes others to pause and ponder as we stand out from the rest of the world, loving everyone, even our enemy. We are salt and light in a decaying and dark world. We are meek and merciful, trustworthy and willing to turn the other cheek. We are faithful in all relationships, in thought and deed. We seek peace and unity where there is division, and rejoice in the reward that awaits us when we are persecuted for our righteousness.

These are lessons that we get to put into practice throughout life. They come in the form of opportunities to stand up and stand out and to walk in faith, being conformed in the image of Christ—perfect.

Lord, make me perfect, complete in
your character and love. Amen.

Never Go Hungry

"For the bread of God is the bread that comes down
from heaven and gives life to the world." ... Jesus declared,
"I am the bread of life. He who comes to me will never
go hungry, and he who believes in me will never be thirsty."
–JOHN 6:33–35 NIV

Think about your comfort foods. Are they sweet or salty? Are you more of a retail therapy person, or do you search for significance at the busyness buffet? Sadly, there is no real fulfillment in any of these indulgences. In fact, they usually result in a gut full of guilt—for how much we just ate, spent, or didn't get done. We are hungry for something, but we just can't seem to put our finger on what it is.

We are craving Christ. We were all created to need Him, but do we get our recommended daily allowance of Him? We need a "divine diet," to turn to His Word or to prayer when the world turns on the pressure. "Cultural casserole" or "secular succotash" won't comfort, quiet, or fix our problems; only Jesus promises to satisfy us.

Jesus, you are always what I need.
The "comforts" of this world are just a snack,
not my Savior. Amen.

Fear Him

For as high as the heavens are above the earth,
so great is his love for those who fear him.
—PSALM 103:11 NIV

In today's Scripture, we are reminded to fear the Lord. This time the word *fear* is the transliterated Hebrew word *yare'*, meaning to inspire reverence, awe, and honor.

We may say things like, "I fear the unknown." That fear fills us with dread or anxiety. On the other hand, fear of the Lord is inspired; it develops and matures as we grow in our relationship with Jesus and know Him. Our awe-inspiring honor of Him grows with that clearer vision of Him.

When we operate in the fear of the Lord, we obey Him and don't worry or fear the consequences. Places that were once filled with fear are flooded with faith in the security of His love. Take some time this week to pray about the things that make you fearful. Let His love hem you in and hold you close.

Lord, help me to overcome my fears with
the fear of you. Fill me with your love. Amen.

Certain, Part 1

Then Caleb silenced the people before Moses and said,
"We should go up and take possession of the land, for we
can certainly do it." … They said, "The land we explored
devours those living in it. All the people we saw there
are of great size. … We seemed like grasshoppers."
—NUMBERS 13:30, 32–33 NIV

Twelve men were sent to spy in the land God had promised to
Moses and the Israelites. God vowed to give them the land,
and sent an angel ahead to drive out the "giants," but somehow
the people forgot His important promise. Ten of the twelve came
back and reported, "We can't," but Caleb and Joshua said, "We
certainly can."

We know the rest of the story: God was furious and swore
that none of them, except Joshua and Caleb, would enter into the
land He promised because they did not believe.

What promises has God given to you? The Bible is filled with
them! We also have our own "giants": temptations, finances, challenging relationships and students, and illness. Name a "giant"
you have struggled with or are currently up against. Now, recite
your favorite promise from Scripture with certainty.

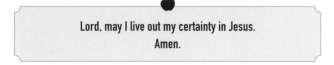

Lord, may I live out my certainty in Jesus.
Amen.

Certain, Part 2

"If the LORD is pleased with us, then He will bring us
into this land and give it to us ... and do not fear the
people of the land, for they will be our prey.
Their protection has been removed from them, and the
LORD is with us; do not fear them." But all the congregation
said to stone them with stones. –NUMBERS 14:8–10

Yesterday we read about Caleb being certain that God would keep His promises and that no giant could stop God. Caleb and Joshua continued to implore the people to trust God, and in return for their encouragement, the people wanted to kill them.

Your students have their "giants" too. Peer pressure is at an epidemic level in elementary as well as secondary schools. "Giants" like drugs, alcohol, sex, cheating, lying, and stealing all stem from the pressure for acceptance, success, and stuff. The desire for cell phones, technology, clothes, and cars surround them and tempt them to give in.

You can help your students overcome their giants. Consider sponsoring a faith club on your campus; there are dozens of great ones to choose from. Share your certainty, and receive all He has promised.

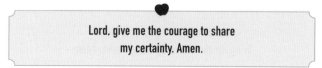

Lord, give me the courage to share
my certainty. Amen.

At the Name

At the name of Jesus every knee should bow, in heaven
and on earth and under the earth, and every tongue confess
that Jesus Christ is Lord, to the glory of God the Father.
—PHILIPPIANS 2:9–11 NIV

Years ago, one of my daughter's church camp counselors, Harvey, told us a story. The camp pool had a diving board, and when he was about to dive in, the kids began to loudly chant his name. Having never felt like that before, this man in his fifties cannon-balled off the diving board, splashing all the laughing campers. But the most delighted person was Harvey!

Do you think he had one good splash and then grabbed his towel and went back to his cabin? Of course not! One good splash deserved another, and another, and another. The campers chanted his name, and cheers erupted with every jump.

What area of your life needs some encouragement right now? A situation at school, or an issue with your family, health, finances, or even faith? Maybe you can't put your finger on what is wrong; you're just in a slump and can't seem to get out. If so, do some chanting of your own and call on the name of Jesus. Nothing surpasses the strength He gives!

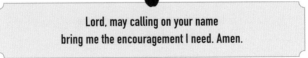

Lord, may calling on your name
bring me the encouragement I need. Amen.

Depart from Danger

Do not be wise in your own eyes; fear the LORD
and depart from evil. –PROVERBS 3:7 NKJV

I wondered why a frog was flying through my yard, until I saw a snake chasing it. The poor thing was hopping for its life. Scripture says we are to flee from sin, turn from temptation, and run to God for refuge, and we would be wise if we followed these instructions with the same energy as that frog.

Do you see your students flirting with temptation or drowning in sinful situations? Or perhaps you're the one struggling. What happens when we ignore warning cries of friends and family or the prompting of the Holy Spirit? We end up wrapped in the clutches of sin, like a boa constrictor's lunch.

If you find yourself sneaking somewhere or hiding something, you're experiencing the staying power of sin. If sin and satan were as scary as that snake was to the frog, there would be no problem; we would recognize them and run for our lives. But sin comes in many packages, and some seem beautiful, desirable, fun, and fulfilling. Beware. Sin is never worth its price!

**Lord, may I always run away
from temptation and sin. Amen.**

My Hope Is in You

May your unfailing love be with us, O LORD,
even as we put our hope in you. —PSALM 33:22 NIV

*H*ope is sometimes confusing and misunderstood. As Christians, we do not put our hope in the things of this world. We do not hope *that* … Instead, we hope *in* the Lord. Christ is the living essence, expectation, and expression of our eternal hope. We put our confidence for life and blessing, both eternally and here on this earth, in Christ. It is how we manage to get out of the bed each morning to face another day, and it is how we lay our heads down and rest through the night—by knowing Christ reigns, even when the world seems out of control.

If we look with earthly eyes at earthly circumstances, we may not have an expectation for good things to come our way. If we look through the eyes of our heart poured out in prayer, knowing where our hope comes from, then we have the promise of peace, purpose, perseverance, and eternal prosperity that will outlast any problem on this earth.

Jesus, you are my hope, today and always.
Amen.

Fearless

"Do not fear, for I am with you; do not anxiously
look about you, for I am your God. I will strengthen you,
surely I will help you, surely I will uphold you with
My righteous right hand." —ISAIAH 41:10

Many people have a fear of failure. They're scared to take risks because they might not succeed or could embarrass themselves or lose relationships. We Christians often feel the same way. What if we say or do the wrong thing? Or if we embarrass or let God down?

We fear because satan is a liar and we are paralyzed by lies. Satan tells us that God abandons us, and that we do not have what it takes. Satan tries to convince us that our future is totally in our hands and we are destined to make a mess of it. All lies! God will never leave us or forsake us. He wants our obedience, and He will take care of our abilities.

What lie has satan been telling you? And what lies has satan been telling your students? They fear failure, losing relationships, and their uncertain future. Sound familiar? Sometimes we have more in common with them than we think.

> Lord, help me to banish satan's lies from
> my life and the lives of those around me. Amen.

Peaceful

The Lord is at hand; do not be anxious about anything,
but in everything by prayer and supplication with
thanksgiving let your requests be made known to God.
And the peace of God, which surpasses all understanding,
will guard your hearts and your minds in Christ Jesus.
—PHILIPPIANS 4:5–7 ESV

People react to stress in a variety of ways. Some get short-tempered, while some get sensitive or even over-sensitive by lashing out in anger or withdrawing in tears. Think about your reaction to tribulation. Would it be considered peaceful, with your emotions and actions remaining calm, collected, and courageous?

Now think about the last great need or challenge you faced. Did you thank God for it? He tells us in His Word that we can be guarded by a peace that "surpasses all understanding" if we put our life and all its circumstances in Christ's hands through prayer and thank Him.

Be thankful for every opportunity to share your faith and hope, which is founded in Christ alone. Fix your eyes on His faithfulness, and let His peace fill the places that fear and worry try to occupy. Do not reside in anxiousness, but abide in Him.

> Lord, you are my peace when
> I face troubling times. Amen.

Love That Surpasses Knowledge

I pray that you, being rooted and established in love, may
have power, together with all the saints, to grasp how wide
and long and high and deep is the love of Christ, and to
know this love that surpasses knowledge—that you may be
filled to the measure of all the fullness of God.

—EPHESIANS 3:17–19 NIV

I pray for teachers every day. I do this because I believe, as has
been said, that, "When we work, we work; but when we pray,
God works."

Prayer is an essential piece of our relationship with God, just
as communication is vital in any relationship. Satan tricks us into
all kinds of excuses, and we start thinking, *I got myself into this mess,
so I have to get myself out*, or *God doesn't want to hear about this problem*.

God's great love for you is immeasurable and indestructible.
If it matters to you, you can be assured that it matters to Him. Lift
up a prayer so that He can lift you up.

Lord, I pray for the power to know this love
that surpasses knowledge, that I may be filled
to the measure of all the fullness of you. Amen.

Source

Son though he was, he learned obedience from what he
suffered and, once made perfect, he became the source of
eternal salvation for all who obey him. –HEBREWS 5:8–9 NIV

Teresa and I stood in my driveway with her car hood open,
trying to figure out why her car wouldn't start. Neither one
of us knew a thing about cars except how to put gas in them.
As my grandfather used to say, "It was like a hog staring at a
wristwatch." Miraculously, we discovered that one of the battery
connectors had pulled out just slightly. We pushed it back in and
tightened the nut and then the car started like it was supposed to.

The battery is the source of electricity, changed into useful
voltage in vehicles; for people, Jesus is the Source that sustains
and saves. You need to keep your motor running as you tend to a
constant pull of responsibilities and needs. Your connection with
Him must remain tight and secure; let suffering strengthen your
connection with Him so that you run at peak performance.

> Lord, may I always stay connected to the Source.
> Amen.

Have Hope

And not only this, but we also exult in our tribulations,
knowing that tribulation brings about perseverance;
and perseverance, proven character; and proven character,
hope; and hope does not disappoint. –ROMANS 5:3–5

We all respond differently to difficult decisions and situations. Perhaps you know someone who runs toward the trouble when everyone else is running away. What do you think gives that person the tenacity to tackle trouble, tribulation, trauma, or tragedy head-on?

Tribulation brings about perseverance—in life, marriage, career, parenting, and so on. We have to resolve to learn from the hard times, not leave. Quitters will never know the blessings they missed by running from a challenge. Grumblers will never grow, because their complaining steals too much time and energy.

We always have a choice—to be hopeless or hopeful. Remember, hope never disappoints. Hope is faith in a Person, not a wish upon a star, and Jesus is our hope. Because of our faith in Jesus, His love pumps through our hearts. Christ's love trumps personality, circumstances, experience, knowledge, earthly wealth, and resources.

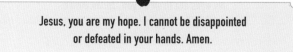

Jesus, you are my hope. I cannot be disappointed
or defeated in your hands. Amen.

Run the Race with Endurance and Grace

> Therefore, since we have so great a cloud of witnesses surrounding us, let us also lay aside every encumbrance and the sin which so easily entangles us, and let us run with endurance the race that is set before us, fixing our eyes on Jesus, the author and perfecter of faith. —HEBREWS 12:1–2

The writer of Hebrews encourages believers in Christ to run with energy, endurance, and effectiveness. Following this advice, we can go from encumbered to energetic and from entangled to enduring.

You are prepared in prayer, and your team stands with you, ready to race with you. You faithfully fix your eyes on Jesus, the One who was faithful before you and blazed the path for you to follow. You resolve not to lose heart and not to grow weary, but to move at the speed of Christ with supernatural strength. You will not shrink back, sit down, or give up, but rather persevere in the presence, power, provision, protection, and promises of almighty God.

Lord, I am focused on the big picture—the kingdom plan. My eyes are fixed on you, Jesus. Amen.

ABOUT THE AUTHOR

Kathy Branzell is the National Coordinator of LOVE2020 and has been an active member of the Mission America Coalition since 2000, serving with the Education Coalition. She taught for ten years in elementary schools (private and public) and then taught in the education departments at the University of Georgia and Fayetteville State University.

Kathy began her ministry journey as the founder and president of Fellowship and Christian Encouragement (FACE) for Educators, where for over seventeen years she has written weekly devotionals to equip and encourage educators. FACE has grown to over 130,000 public and private school educators as they meet and pray in their schools each week. Her writings and prayers are based on the conversations and hundreds of prayer requests she receives each week from educators across the US and worldwide.

Kathy serves on the Board and Membership of the National Prayer Committee. She also sits on the Board of Directors for The National Day of Prayer (NDP), where she coordinates partnerships and philanthropy and helped organize events for the Pray for America Bus Tours from 2013–2015. The 2015 bus tour went to fifty-two college and university campuses in fifty-six days as well as homeschool and high school campuses; the NDP bus team prayed with educators from pre-K through college.

Kathy is the author of the book *Prayer Warrior: The Battle Plan to Victory* and is a contributing author for the book *The Front Line*. She is also a chaplain for the Billy Graham Evangelistic Association Rapid Response Team.

Kathy earned her bachelor's degree in education and human development from the University of Georgia and went on to earn a master's degree in biblical studies from Liberty Theological Seminary.

She is the wife to her childhood sweetheart, Russ, and mom to Chandler and Emily.

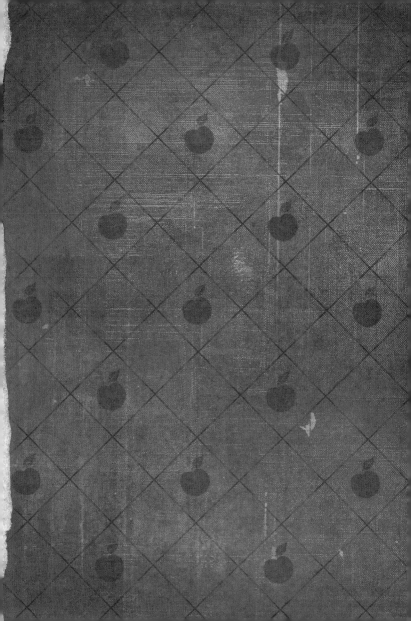

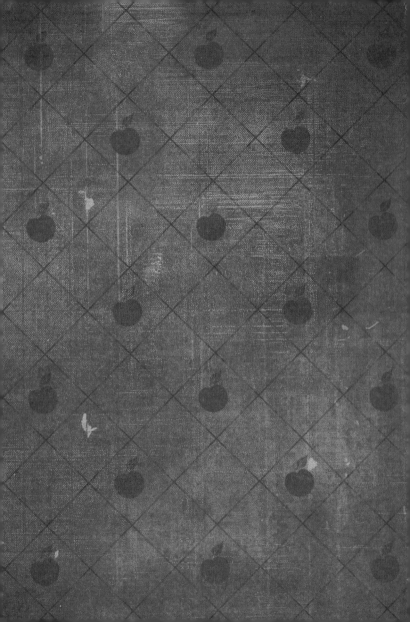